In rereading E. Stanley Jones's *The Christ of the Indian Road*, so many of his ideas still stand up, even one hundred years after it was first written. Indeed, in many ways the book was ahead of its time. I especially appreciate Jones's focus on the person of Christ instead of a doctrinal approach to Christianity, his emphasis on the importance of religious experience, and his insistence on appreciating the spiritual gifts of every culture. These three ideas resonate with the teachings of Father Richard Rohr, who has had a profound impact on my life. They also have implications for the work of Global Ministries of The United Methodist Church, which I lead. In our work at Global Ministries, including The United Methodist Committee on Relief (UMCOR), we are seeking to better understand how the perspectives of partners from many national and cultural backgrounds can inform our work, even if that means shifting away from some of our inherited forms and structures. And I have emphasized to our staff and board the necessity of a strong spiritual grounding to keep us engaged in making our contribution to God's mission, just as we joyfully welcome the contributions of people from other religious traditions and cultures. I hope that Jones's reflections will continue to challenge and provoke other Christians as they seek to faithfully follow Jesus in this present age.

—**Roland Fernandes**

General Secretary of the General Board of Global Ministries, including UMCOR, and General Board of Higher Education and Ministry, The United Methodist Church

Jesus is Lord!

Grace and peace be unto you in the blessed name of our dear Lord Jesus Christ!

It gives me immense joy to write a few lines about this new and enhanced version of *The Christ of the Indian Road,* first published in 1925. E. Stanley Jones needs no introduction to his writings and ministry; it would be like showing light to the sun. Millions of copies of his books have been sold worldwide and are still being widely read.

E. Stanley Jones, the founder of Sat Tal Christian Ashram in Nainital, India, expresses that Christianity is founded on the laws of the kingdom of God (a phrase that Jesus used more than one hundred times in his teachings), and that the kingdom of God is built into the nature of the universe and into the nature of humanity. The kingdom of God teaches the survival of the fittest, and in a moral and spiritual universe, the morally and spiritually fit survive and pass on their spiritual and physical qualities to the next generation. When in times of moral and spiritual decay and challenge, we need Christianity to return to Jesus's emphasis on the kingdom of God or we risk the moral and spiritual fitness of our future generations. The kingdom of God was a major focus of Jones's preaching and evangelism, and the church would be wise to return to an emphasis on God's kingdom.

Stanley Jones's teaching, preaching, and writing on mission and evangelism were unparalleled during his many decades in India and have an impact to this day. In his book *The Christ of the Indian Road,* E. Stanley Jones reaches out to persons in India without denouncing or attacking their religions and presents Christ as naturalized in India, the answer to all human need, the Christ of the Indian Road. Jones makes it clear that Christianity must be defined as Christ, not the Old Testament, not Western civilization, not even the system built around him in the West, but Christ himself, and to be a Christian is to follow him.

This book, amongst others written by Jones, helps people understand that Jesus is above religion and relatable and available to any person seeking God. E. Stanley Jones, through his missionary experience, learned that people were more interested in Jesus than "Christianity" and were open to hearing about Him. This remains true today in India and across the world. Seeking persons will find that the life and ministry of Jesus Christ is the source for answers to their questions, the only source. The doctrine and teachings of the Lord Jesus Christ are supreme and must be given precedence. Once we turn toward Jesus, I believe that Christ's followers will experience a vibrant Christianity that is available to all.

We hope and pray that the thoughts of E. Stanley Jones in his book *The Christ of the Indian Road* will produce a powerful testimony for practicing Christians—to understand that the Kingdom of God is present on earth now, not just something only in the hereafter. Jones shares with his readers the reality of the Kingdom of God for them, and for them now.

Having completed his life on earth, fulfilling God's path, E. Stanley Jones breathed his last on January 25, 1973, in Bareilly, Uttar Pradesh, an area often considered the bastion of the Methodist Church in India and in later years became known as part of the "Methodist trail." Jones's grave should be marked with a flame of glory!

I extend my best wishes and gratitude to The United Methodist Publishing House for this centennial anniversary publication, as well as to the Christian community at large. I exhort and encourage one and all to pick up a copy today and read through the precious works of this great missionary and evangelist, who was guided by the gospel and followed Jesus.

—**Bishop Dr. Anilkumar John Servand**

Chief Acharya, Sat Tal Christian Ashram, Nainital

Bishop, Mumbai & North India Regional Conferences,

The Methodist Church in India

Master and President, Serampore College (University)

Central Committee Member, World Council of Churches

The Christ of the Indian Road

The Christ of the Indian Road

E. Stanley Jones

Edited by
Anne Mathews-Younes
and Mathew Thattamannil Thomas

Abingdon Press | Nashville

The Christ of the Indian Road

ISBN: 978-1-791-03515-0

MANUFACTURED IN THE UNITED STATES OF AMERICA

CONTENTS

Notes from the Editors

Anne Mathews-Younes
and Mathew Thattamannil Thomas

The idea of the universal Christ was the foundation for Jones's first book, *The Christ of the Indian Road* (1925), which was his effort to create a more culturally inclusive vision of Christianity in which he preached a "disentangled Christ," differentiated from Western civilization and unspiritual Europeanism.[1] Jones believed that India could have Christ without Western civilization. He made the case that Indian philosophical structures were as valid as Greco-Roman philosophy for framing an articulation of the gospel. He asserted

1. Stephen A. Graham, *Ordinary Man, Extraordinary Mission: The Life and Work of E. Stanley Jones* (Nashville: Abingdon Press, 2005), 149. In his autobiography, Jones relished this particular illustration of the impact on India of the disentangled Christ. He writes:

> A Hindu principal of a college was chairman of one of my meetings and in his closing remarks he said: "Jesus has stood four times before the door of India and has knocked. The first time he appeared he stood in the company of a trader. He knocked. We looked out and saw him and liked him, but we didn't like his company, so we shut the door. Later he appeared, with a diplomat on one side and a soldier on the other, and knocked. We looked out and said, 'We like you, but we don't like your company.' Again we shut the door. The third time was when he appeared as the uplifter of the outcastes. We like him better in this role, but we weren't sure of what was behind it. Was this the religious side of imperialism? Are they conquering us through religion? Again we shut the door. And now he appears before our doors, as tonight, as the disentangled Christ. To this disentangled Christ we say: 'Come in. Our doors are open to you'" (*A Song of Ascents: A Spiritual Autobiography* (Nashville: Abingdon Press, 2018), 110).

that this Greco-Roman Western perspective would limit the capacity for Christianity to be naturalized in India. Instead, we should look to India to develop the capacity to universalize Christianity. He writes in *The Christ of the Indian Road*:

> The religious genius of India is the richest in the world. . . . As that genius pours itself into Christian molds it will enrich the collective expression of Christianity. But to do that the Indian must remain Indian. He must stand in the stream of India's culture and life and let the force of that stream go through his soul so that the expression of his Christianity will be essentially Eastern and not Western. (208)[2]

Stephen Graham, a biographer of Jones, writes:

> *The Christ of the Indian Road* was a frontal assault on the cultural prejudices of most European and American Christian missionaries in the late nineteenth and early twentieth centuries. Jones was one of the first Western Christians to realize that in Asia, Africa, and Latin America the Christian gospel was often betrayed by being enmeshed with the economic and political self-aggrandizement of Western nations. In so doing, Jones declared his moral and intellectual independence from Western political and religious imperialism.[3]

Jones was a careful student of Indian culture and was sensitive to the impact of his presence as a missionary. According to Graham, Jones was aware of what was going on in India, both spiritually and politically. Jones internalized and used his "awareness" and called for all Western Christians in India, beginning with himself, to be more sensitive to the spirit of Jesus Christ in their adopted country. Jones perhaps surprised

2. All parenthetical citations here and in the following essays are from this edition of *The Christ of the Indian Road*.

3. Graham, *Ordinary Man*, 159.

many of his Western Christian colleagues, as he recognized the presence of the Holy Spirit in the most unfamiliar places and in the most unexpected ways as he continued to discover the Christian truth in Hindu theology.[4]

The Christ of the Indian Road had a profound impact on Christian missions and now, at the one hundredth anniversary of the initial publication of this outstanding book, we wish to reissue it and include commentary from leading Indian scholars of Christian missions. Some language in the original text has been updated to be more culturally appropriate in today's context and slight edits were made for clarity.

Dr. Anne Mathews-Younes, granddaughter of renowned missionary, author, and evangelist Dr. E. Stanley Jones, is the president of the E. Stanley Jones Foundation. She is dedicated to continuing her grandfather's legacy of sharing the life-transforming message of Jesus Christ and equipping others for effective Christian evangelism.

Mathews-Younes earned her master's and doctoral degrees in theological studies from Wesley Theological Seminary in Washington, DC, and traveled extensively with him through India and Africa. Under her leadership, the E. Stanley Jones Foundation works to make Jones's Christ-centered teachings and writings accessible to new generations. In partnership with Abingdon Press, the Foundation is reprinting all twenty-seven of his books in 2025 to commemorate the one hundredth anniversary of their continuous publication.

As an internationally recognized speaker, she frequently presents in countries where E. Stanley Jones's impact endures, including India, Japan, Korea, Canada, and the Americas. She was deeply influenced by attending the Mar Thoma Convention

4. Graham, *Ordinary Man*, 167.

with her grandfather in 1967. She returned to the Convention as a speaker in 2016 and 2019 and delivered the keynote address at the centennial celebration of the Sevika Sanghom, the largest women's Christian service organization in the Mar Thoma Church, with over two hundred thousand attendees.

Dr. Mathew Thattamannil Thomas is a member of the Mar Thoma Church and resides in Maryland, USA. Thomas has held several active leadership positions within the Mar Thoma Church Diocese of North America. He was a member of the Diocesan Council for nine years (2008 to 2016) and the chief editor of the quarterly Diocesan magazine, The Mar Thoma Messenger, *for ten years, and has contributed as an author and editor to other books and studies. He continues to serve the Mar Thoma Church of Greater Washington in leadership roles.*

Thomas also offers leadership in the Ecumenical Council of Kerala Christians (ECKC; first president 1991, president 2021, and treasurer 2023), which now includes sixteen Christian churches from Kerala, India, with branches in Washington DC, Maryland, and Virginia. He migrated to the United States of America in 1983 soon after completing his medical education from the Medical College under the University of Madras. He worked more than thirty-four years for the US Food and Drug Administration (FDA), including as a senior diplomat at the US Embassy in New Delhi as the country director for the US FDA India Office and as the US DHHS health attaché. He continues to work as an independent clinical-research and regulatory consultant for medical products development through his firm, MTT Consulting LLC., and as a consultant and expert trainer for The Way Consulting International, a subsidiary of the E. Stanley Jones Foundation, that focuses on training faith leaders for suicide prevention.

Foreword

Leonard Sweet

Life is a series of missed moments, or seized moments.

Take the case of Professor Martin Luther King Jr. In 1959, the president of Morehouse College Dr. Benjamin Mays persuaded King to teach a course at his alma mater and to spread the message of the civil rights movement to students. Philosophy professor Samuel Williams was assigned to assist King to make it easier for him to fit this course into his brutal schedule during the academic year of 1959–1960.

Only eight students signed up. These eight students, including Julian Bond, Amos Brown, John Lewis, and Prathia Hall Wynn, are the only people who can claim, "Dr. King was my professor." They are the only ones who can claim, "I was a student of Martin Luther King Jr." They are the only ones who can call Dr. King their academic mentor. But even though these elite eight had the good sense to take the course and seize the moment, they still missed their moment: not one of them saved the syllabus; not one of them took a picture with their professor; not one of them saved any of his signed evaluations of their work. In words from T. S. Eliot's *Four Quartets*, "We had the experience but missed the meaning."[1]

1. T. S. Eliot, "The Dry Salvages," *Four Quartets* (New York: Harcourt, 1943), lines 16–17.

The syllabus for King's course, "Social Philosophy," included readings from the greatest thinkers in political theory, such as John Stuart Mill, Hegel, Rousseau, Socrates, Plato, and more. The final exam posed the question of whether Adam Smith or Karl Marx would support the nonviolent theory of social change. The course also covered topics like Thoreau's philosophy of civil disobedience, the theory and practice of different civil rights movements, and most particularly, a case study of Gandhi's nonviolent resistance, called *satyagraha*. King and his wife, Coretta, had returned earlier that year from a five-week trip to India (3 February–13 March 1959), so Gandhi's philosophy was fresh on King's mind.

How did King become so familiar with, and enamored of, Gandhi's philosophy of nonviolent resistance? King credited E. Stanley Jones and Jones's discussion of Gandhi as a key influence on his embrace of nonviolence in the civil rights movement. In a 1957 interview with *Ebony* magazine, King stated: "I looked at Gandhi, at his method, as the only morally and practically sound method open to oppressed people in their struggle for freedom." And in a direct reference to Jones's book, King said:

> It was in this Gandhian emphasis on love and nonviolence that I discovered the method for social reform that I had been seeking for so many months. The reverend Mr. Jones was the first to bring the message of Gandhi to our struggle through his *Christ of the Indian Road*.[2]

At a 1964 Boston University reception in King's honor, King also confessed privately to Eunice Mathews, daughter of

2. King went on to explain that Gandhi's campaigns of nonviolent resistance greatly fascinated him. "I came to see for the first time that the Christian doctrine of love operating through the Gandhian method of nonviolence was one of the most potent weapons available to an oppressed people in their struggle for freedom." See Lerone Bennett Jr., "Interview with Martin Luther King," *Ebony*, September 1957, 23–26.

Methodist missionary and theologian E. Stanley Jones, that it was her father's introduction to Gandhi that provided him with a spiritual and theological framework for nonviolence. It was Jones's filtering of his friend Gandhi's concept of *satyagraha* (nonviolent resistance) that showed King how Christ's emphasis on love, even for enemies, could be a potent force against oppression. It was this book that opened the door to the centerpiece doctrine of the civil rights movement, which opened the door to one of the most important social movements of the twentieth century, which opened the door to greater equality, opportunity, and inclusion for historically oppressed groups while also revealing the depth of systemic injustices that are still being reckoned with today.

When King read Jones's biography of Gandhi, he highlighted the following section of the book and wrote in the margin, "This is it, the way to win freedom for the Negro in America!":

> But the Mahatma repudiated with all his might the idea that the method of trust and nonviolence was used because he was weak and cowardly. He insisted that it was the method of the strong, and only the method of the strong. He further insisted that it was better to fight than to take up nonviolence through fear or cowardice.
>
> The weapons Gandhi chose were simple: We will match our capacity to suffer against your capacity to inflict the suffering, our soul force against your physical force. We will not hate you, but we will not obey you. Do what you like, and we will wear you down by our capacity to suffer. And in the winning of freedom, we will so appeal to your heart and conscience that we will win you. So ours will be a double victory; we will win our freedom and our captors in the process.[3]

3. E. Stanley Jones, *Gandhi: Portrait of a Friend* (Nashville: Abingdon Press, 2019), 77.

King's highlighted copy of Jones's book is on display at the King Center library in Atlanta.

If there were an award for the most influential but uncelebrated book, *The Christ of the Indian Road* would be in the top five. The book presented a compelling reinterpretation of Christ through the lens of Indian thought. Jones showed how the principles of love and nonviolence central to Christ's message resonated with Hindu concepts, inspiring missiologists to bridge divides between Christianity and other religions. The book is a classic in contextual theology and inculturation. It inspired many initiatives in creative, culturally adaptive evangelism.

If there were an award for the most influential but uncelebrated Christian leader of the twentieth century, E. Stanley Jones might be no. 1. A 1938 issue of *Time* named the fifty-three-year-old Jones "the world's greatest Christian missionary."[4] A case could be made that he was the world's greatest missionary since the apostle Paul. Gandhi and Jones met in 1929, when Gandhi participated in a round table conference organized by Jones to promote interfaith dialogue. This began their longtime friendship and Jones's embrace of Gandhi's method of *satyagraha* as a means of social and political change. Gandhi and Jones traveled together as well, and Jones was actually due to meet with Gandhi on the day of his assassination in 1948. Instead, word of the tragedy reached him while en route. Devastated, Jones poured his grief into a two-month writing spree that produced a best-selling biography of Gandhi (*Mahatma Gandhi: An Interpretation*, reprinted in 2019 as *Gandhi: Portrait of a Friend*) that helped spread Gandhi's influence around the world.

Jones broadened Christian missionary approaches and highlighted the importance of respectful dialogue with other

4. "Religion: One Hope," *Time*, December 12, 1938.

faiths, recognizing the potential for a deeper, more inclusive understanding of Christianity in different cultural contexts. Without the writings and work of E. Stanley Jones, you can't understand the theology of three of the most prominent postcolonial missiologists of the twentieth century: the South African David Bosch, the Briton Andrew Walls, and the American Gerald H. Anderson.

I personally experienced the lingering impact of Jones's influence when I was asked to speak at the Maramon Convention (Kerala, India), the largest annual gathering of Christians in Asia. Jones was a regular speaker at Maramon from the 1920s into the 1960s. His deep friendships with leaders of the Mar Thoma Syrian Church, cultivated over some fifty trips to India, and his deep respect for Indian thought and culture made him a welcome and recurring figure—to the point where even Hindus began calling him *rishi* (a saint). His sainthood resounds even today in Indian circles, especially Maramon.

There is a story about Gandhi reading *The Christ of the Indian Road,* though I have not been able to find definitive documentary evidence for it. Upon completing it, Gandhi was said to have closed the book and remarked to Jones, "Though I do not agree with all you say, I think it needs to be read by all of India."

I agree with Gandhi but go further. *The Christ of the Indian Road* offers profound insights into the intersection of spirituality, culture, and the human experience. Its messages transcend geographical boundaries and have the potential to resonate with people from all walks of life. By exploring the book's themes, readers across the globe can gain a deeper understanding of their own spiritual journeys and the ways in which faith can unite humanity. For these reasons, I believe *The Christ of the Indian Road* needs to be read by all the world.

Sometimes we miss our moments. Sometimes we seize the moment. My heartfelt hope is that this moment, celebrating the centennial of a truly remarkable book, will seize you. May it inspire you to delve into the pages of *The Christ of the Indian Road*, to grapple with its profound truths, and to emerge transfixed and transfigured by its message. Its timeless wisdom and profound insights remain even more relevant today than they were a century ago. Let us not miss this moment.

Leonard Sweet is a theo-semiotician, historical theologian, and preacher who grew up with two brothers under a preacher-mom (see Mother Tongue*). Author of almost eighty books, hundreds of articles, and almost two thousand published sermons, his most recent publications include his lifelong semiotic study of the Jesus story,* Jesus Human and Designer Jesus, *as well as an introductory textbook on theo-semiotics,* Decoding the Divine. *His pastoral sensibilities are currently evident in* The Sound of Light *(with Lisa Samson) and an upcoming* The Advent Adventure *book of meditations. His semiotic "LenTalks" are posted on YouTube, and his "Napkin Scribbles" podcasts can be accessed on leonardsweet.com or Spotify. After a lifetime in academic administration as dean, provost, president, and chancellor, Sweet now works with graduate students at four institutions: Drew University, where he has occupied the E. Stanley Jones Chair, George Fox University, Northwind Seminary, and Southeastern University. A sought-after speaker in the religious world today, he and his family reside on Orcas Island in the San Juan Islands, where they operate a hospitality resort (or "advance center") called Sanctuary Seaside. His next book (with Chris Eriksen) is a theology of football called* Gridiron Gospel: Faith That Moves Chains.

The Lingering Message of E. Stanley Jones

Most Rev. Dr. Theodosius
Mar Thoma Metropolitan

Jesus does not need to be protected. He needs to be presented.

—E. Stanley Jones, *The Christ of the Indian Road*

Introduction

E. Stanley Jones (1884–1973) was a missionary with a difference in so far as he tried to relate the gospel of Jesus Christ to the sociopolitical and cultural realities of India. Born in Baltimore, Maryland, United States, he reached India as a Methodist missionary in 1907—a period when the nationalist movement in the country was at its peak. Convinced that self-determination was crucial for the Indians, Jones challenged the thousands of Western missionaries in India to develop a deep sensitivity to the context in which they worked. He also entered into dialogue with the nationalist leaders of India, urging them to be more open to Christian missions. Jones passed away on January 25, 1973, at Bareilly, Uttar Pradesh, India.

In his commitment to be a witness to Jesus the Christ with openness to all, and under the guidance of the Holy Spirit,

Jones became a friend of many churches in India and very especially to the Malankara Mar Thoma Syrian Church. He was inspired and became inspirational in the gospel sharing and socially transforming meeting that the Mar Thoma Church organized and continues to organize on the banks of the Pamba River in Maramon, Kerala. Popularly known as the Maramon Convention, this annual week-long event remains the biggest Christian gathering in Asia, hosting people of all Christian persuasions and other religions. For Jones, the convention provides Syrian Christians, who as he notes had hitherto been considered "dead for centuries," a new impetus. "They are now beginning to be keen and alive and the largest Christian audience in the world gathers at the time of the yearly convention, when in a single audience there will be thirty-five thousand people. These conventions have been marked with great spiritual power, and the church is now beginning to take its place in the evangelization of India" (125). The Maramon Convention became the umbilical bond between Dr. E. Stanley Jones and the Mar Thoma Church, and he became a regular preacher at the Maramon Convention for decades and contributed to the growth and reach of the Convention and the ministry of the Mar Thoma Church as a whole. In fact, this relationship continued on with his next generation as well. The Mar Thoma Church is greatly indebted to Dr. E. Stanley Jones.

Besides being a profound gospel preacher, Stanley Jones was a prolific writer, authoring a number of books and articles. Several of his books discuss the meaning of Christ in the Indian context. The need to contextualize Christianity in India was the subject of his seminal work, *The Christ of the Indian Road*, which sold more than one million copies worldwide after its publication in 1925. The book discusses several topics relevant at that time, such as the message of Mahatma Gandhi, Christianity and other religions, and relevant patterns of Christian witness in the pluralistic context of India. As the author notes in the preface to the book, "Perhaps a few words of caution may be helpful to the reader. To those familiar with India the title of this volume may lead the reader to expect the book to be what it is not—an Indian interpretation of Christ. It is, rather, an attempt to describe how Christ is becoming naturalized upon the Indian Road. The Indian interpretation of Christ must be left to later hands" (63).

A century later, when we consider the relevance of *The Christ of the Indian Road*, several questions come to mind. Considering India's slide into a more authoritarian and Hindu nationalist direction, what would be the motive of Christian mission in this country? What are the challenges today as the Christian faith encounters a plethora of religions and ideologies? Has the legacy of Mahatma Gandhi transitioned from being the leading figure of the independence movement to an ideal and an ideology? What does it mean to be a Christian in India today? This essay will briefly address some of these questions.

"The Christ of the Indian Road": The Context

At the outset of the book, Stanley Jones makes it clear that *The Christ of the Indian Road* is different from the stereotypical books written by the Christian missionaries who are obsessed with the problems of India such as caste and poverty. Jones points out that the missionaries, in order to arouse the West to missionary activity, have too often emphasized the dark side of India. While what they have said may have been true, the picture was not an entirely accurate one. "This overemphasis on the one side has often created either pity or contempt in the minds of the hearers. In modern jargon a superiority complex has resulted. I do not believe a superiority complex to be the proper spring for missionary activity" (65). He continuously postured himself as an admirer of the beauty of India and a well-wisher for the possibilities before her through independence and nationalism, and he was hopeful about Christ becoming the transforming source for the nation.

Jones lived and worked in India at a time when the missionary movement was at its zenith in the country. He had a distinct approach in several senses. He refused to caricature Indians as a superstitious and illiterate people. He was sensitive to the cultural and religious diversity of the land and shaped his message around it even while holding to his vocation, like the other missionaries, of converting the people to Christ. In several respects he was a missionary with a difference. As he puts it:

> A friend of mine was talking to a Brahman gentleman when the Brahman turned to him and said, "I don't like the Christ of your creeds and the Christ of your churches." My friend quietly replied, "Then how would you like the Christ of the Indian Road?" The Brahman thought a moment, mentally picturing the Christ of the Indian Road—he saw him dressed in Sadhus' garments, seated by the wayside with the crowds about him, healing blind men who felt their way to him, putting his hands upon the heads of poor, unclean lepers who fell at his feet, announcing the good tidings of the Kingdom to stricken folks, staggering up a lone hill with a broken heart and dying upon a wayside cross for humanity, but rising triumphantly and walking on that road again. He suddenly turned to the friend and earnestly said, "I could love and follow the Christ of the Indian Road." (83)

Citing such anecdotal incidents, Jones took care to distinguish and differentiate Christ of the Indian Road from all baggage of Western culture and even church dogmas and denominationalism.

The Christ of the Indian Road was written at a time when the nationalist movement in India was picking up momentum.

While several Western missionaries considered colonial rule and Christianization two sides of the same coin, Jones was clear that the Christian mission in India was far greater than the rise or fall of the British Empire. In chapter 3 of the book, he narrates an incident that reflected his thinking on the matter:

> A few years ago I was talking to a devoted English missionary who was confused and discouraged about the national situation. She wondered of what use it was to try any more to do Christian work in India since Britain had lost moral hold upon India. There was such bitterness everywhere, and she could feel it. We talked about the inner meaning of things and I told her of what I had seen. I shall never forget the look on her face as she said: "I see the light. Christ is bigger than my empire, and his kingdom may come either through it or in spite of it. I see light bursting through these clouds that have hung over me." A little window had let her see "a great light." (106)

Jones's position on India's desire for independence, his "strong stance on the validity of Indian intellectual and religious structure,"[1] and his friendship with Gandhi may have led to criticism from home but also won him friends and influence among the Hindu population of India. However, the broader legacy of Christian missionaries has continued to haunt the Indian church and its work. The "missionary tag" on Indian Christianity has led to suspicion and hostility among the majority Hindu public of the country. The fact that much of the structures, theology, and liturgy of the Indian church continued to reflect the missionary and colonial heritage contributed significantly to the impression that Christianity is a foreign religion in India. *Christ on the Indian Road* was a call to avoid this danger of Indian Christianity becoming a "pale

1. David Bundy, "The Theology of the Kingdom of God in E. Stanley Jones," *Wesleyan Theological Journal* 23, no. 1–2 (March 1, 1988): 67.

copy" (74) of the Western churches and an invitation to boldly and openly experience Jesus the Person and articulate that Jesus in Indian garb.

The Nationalist Movement of India

Stanley Jones wrote *The Christ of the Indian Road* at a time when Mahatma Gandhi was beginning to play a central role in the nationalist movement of India. Here and in subsequent books, Jones outlines his dialogical relationship with Gandhi. Jones underlined the Christlike behavior of Gandhi and the nationalist movement even as they were involved in civil disobedience and violating the law of the empire. Chapter 4 of *The Christ of the Indian Road* narrates one such instance:

> In one place the nationalists were forbidden by the government to carry the national flag beyond a certain point on a bridge which led into the European or Civil section of the town. The nationalists made it an issue. The magistrate, who arrested and tried most of them, remarked to me that those whom he arrested were much more Christian in their spirit than he was. They would let him know what time they were coming across the bridge with the flag and how many! Would he please be prepared for twenty-five today. Of the twelve hundred who were arrested in that flag agitation, although none of them were professed Christians, and although they could take into jail with them only a limited number of things which they had to produce before the magistrate, the vast majority took New Testaments with them to read while there. The reason they did so becomes apparent when one of them remarked, "We now know what it means for you Christians to suffer for Christ." The cross had become not a doctrine, but a living thing to them. (119)

Jones acknowledged that Gandhi did not call himself a Christian and that he was a Hindu. But by his life, outlook, and methods, Gandhi had been the medium through which a great deal of Indians became interested in Christ. The statement "The cross had become not a doctrine, but a living thing to them" summed up Jones's perception of Gandhi and his followers. He did not go along with the criticism of several Westerners that because many Indians had not converted to Christianity, the Christian mission was a failed project in India. Jones did believe professing Christ as Lord and Savior was the ultimate goal of the mission, but he seemed to argue there were penultimate goals as well. Even though the cross had not become a doctrine for the nationalist leaders, the fact that it was a living thing to them was for Jones not an insignificant goal of the Christian mission.

Discussing Gandhi's pivotal role in shaping the course of India's struggle for independence, Jones adds: "He rejected both the sword and the bomb, not because it was expedient, but because he believed with all his soul in something else, in another type of power—soul force or the power of suffering—and another type of victory—a victory over oneself, this inward victory being the precursor of the outward national victory. In the fires of that suffering there would come the inward freedom, the purification of the social and political life from within" (114).

Encounter with Mahatma Gandhi

Chapter 4 of *The Christ of the Indian Road* bears the title "Jesus Comes through Irregular Channels—Mahatma Gandhi's Part." There is no question E. Stanley Jones had a special relationship with Mahatma Gandhi. The nature of this relationship becomes clearer when we bring in C. F. Andrews, a contemporary of Jones and another Western missionary in India who had a close relationship with Gandhi. M. M. Thomas, in his book *The Acknowledged Christ of the Indian Renaissance*, draws a comparison between the relationship of Andrews and E. Stanley Jones to Gandhi. As Thomas puts it:

> C. F. Andrews belonged to the inner circle of Gandhi's friends. Therefore, his evaluation of Gandhi's theology and views of Christianity have special importance for the Indian people, especially those who have been part of the Gandhian movement in one form or another. But there were Christian evangelists who sought to understand and interpret Gandhi sympathetically from within the orthodoxy of the Christian church, on the basis of their own personal relation with Gandhi and Gandhism. Of such, E. Stanley Jones was foremost. In the introduction to his book on Gandhi he speaks of the thirty years of being at the nerve center of the controversy between Gandhiji and the missionary on the question of conversion.[2]

Thomas goes on to quote Jones, who states, "I am still an evangelist. I bow to Mahatma Gandhi, but I kneel at the feet of Christ and give him my full and final allegiance. And yet a little man, who fought a system in the framework of which I stand, has taught me more of the Spirit of Christ than perhaps any other man in East or West."

Stanley Jones had a long debate with Mahatma Gandhi on the latter's acknowledgment of the principles of Christ but reluctance to accept the person of Christ as Lord and Savior. Jones wrote to Gandhi:

> I thought you had grasped the centre of the Christian faith, but I am afraid I must change my mind. I think you have grasped certain principles of the Christian faith, which have molded you and have helped make

2. M. M. Thomas, *The Acknowledged Christ of the Indian Renaissance* (Chennai: Christian Literature Society, 1968), 228.

> you great—you have grasped the Principles but you have missed the Person. . . . May I suggest that you penetrate through the Principles to the Person and then come back and tell us what you have found. I don't say this as a mere Christian propagandist. I say this because we need you and need the illustration you could give us if you really grasped the centre—the Person.[3]

Gandhi's reply included these words: "I cannot grasp the position by the intellect; the heart must be touched. Saul became Paul, not by an intellectual effort but by something touching his heart. All I can say is that my heart is absolutely open . . . I want to . . . see God face to face. But there I stop."[4]

Jones was convinced that the theology of mission for contemporary India must explore the nature of the acknowledgment of the Person implied in the acknowledgment of the Principle. Gandhi was not prepared to go that far, but that did not diminish Jones's admiration for the Mahatma. He frequently wrote of how Gandhi was closer to Christ than, perhaps, most Christians. Preaching at the Maramon Convention, Jones declared: "Heaven would be poorer without Gandhiji." That was a bold statement for a Christian preacher, especially as many of his listeners held exclusivist evangelical positions. Jones realized that despite all polemic differences, there can be a meeting of the hearts of two earnest seekers, even while they subscribed to divergent theological positions and religious persuasions.

Despite fundamental differences, Jones did not have any hesitation in acknowledging the uniqueness of Gandhi for the soul of India and humanity. He characterized the assassination of the Mahatma as "the greatest tragedy since the Son of God died on a cross." As he put it, Gandhi "marched into

3. Thomas, *The Acknowledged Christ*, 229–230.
4. Thomas, *The Acknowledged Christ*, 229–230.

the soul of humanity in the most triumphal march that any man ever made since the death and resurrection of the Son of God."[5] Jones went on to add that the Mahatma was influenced and molded by Christian principles, particularly the Sermon on the Mount.

Jones concluded his discussion of Gandhi by acknowledging the challenge his life and message posed for Christian mission in India. As he put it, a nationalist leader who was formerly opposed to Christianity said, "I never understood the meaning of Christianity until I saw it in Gandhi." While this inspires us and we are deeply grateful for it, nevertheless, it is a sword that cuts two ways, for some of us have been there all these years and deeply regret that Christianity did not burst into meaning through us. "However, we are glad that India is seeing. And let it be quietly said that we too are seeing" (122).

The Indian Road Led to the Ashram

E. Stanley Jones was a pioneer of the Christian ashram movement. He found ashrams to be a viable means to communicate the Christian message in India. "The ashram, a unique movement based on Indian culture and religion, was adopted by some Indian Christian leaders who, in the twentieth century, began to seek an alternate lifestyle and indigenous ways to practice the Christian faith."[6] Jones believed there should be an Indian way of witnessing to Christ in this pluralistic context, and the ashram was the answer to his quest. The ashram, for him, could be a place for social, political, or religious

5. E. Stanley Jones, *Mahatma Gandhi: An Interpretation* (New York: Abingdon-Cokesbury Press, 1948), 16.

6. A. K. Tharien, "The Ashram Movement" in *The Oxford Encyclopedia of South Asian Christianity* (New Delhi: Oxford University Press, 2012), 40.

purposes. As Richard Taylor describes the Christian ashram movement: "the ashram was to be truly Christian and truly Indian."[7] This model fitted Jones's thinking perfectly. He was convinced that the ashram form of expression was best suited for Christian mission in India.

In 1929 Stanley Jones founded the Sat Tal Ashram in the Nainital District of Uttaranchal (now Uttarakhand) as one of the early Christian ashrams in India. The ashram was modeled very much on Gandhi's own. Spread over an area of over four hundred acres and including a lake and several cottages, the Sat Tal Estate provided the right setting for people to live together, worship together, and dialogue with each other.

Unlike several other ashrams, at Sat Tal there is a strong intellectual side to the discussions, but the basis of all deliberations is moral and spiritual. Groups of people—Christians and people of other faiths, Indians, and foreigners—regularly come there for dialogue with each other. At the Sat Tal Ashram, Stanley Jones attempted the indigenization of mission, drawing people of diverse faith backgrounds to study in-depth their own spiritual natures and what other faiths had to offer. The ashram also facilitates spiritual conferences, workshops, seminars, retreats, and dialogue with other religions. In addition, it runs a school of evangelism and various programs for individuals, families, and churches. The aim of all the deliberations there is to think through problems in an Eastern setting and thus produce a more indigenous expression of the Christian message. Jesus is Lord is the motto of the Sat Tal Ashram. In 2005, the platinum jubilee of the ashram was celebrated, recognizing that over its seventy-five years of ministry, the influence of the Sat Tal Christian Ashram has spread to all parts of the world.

---

7. Richard W. Taylor, "The Legacy of E. Stanley Jones," *International Bulletin of Missionary Research* 6, no. 3 (1982): 104.

Christ and the Other Faiths

The Christ of the Indian Road outlines a number of encounters that E. Stanley Jones had with the Hindu and Muslim scholars and intellectuals of that period. Often, both sides put forth their points of view, striving to reach common ground. A century back, dialogue—or encounter—was a mode of Christian witness in which one strove to argue and prove the legitimacy of one's position. Jones, too, like other scholars of that period, was often seen trying to intellectually convince his opponent of his position. It is, however, important to note that he played an important role at a crucial phase in the history of India. After B. R. Ambedkar's declaration in 1935 that he would reject Hinduism because of discrimination on the basis of caste, Jones and the other Christian leaders met him and invited him to accept the Christian faith. However, realizing Indian Christianity also was divided on caste lines, Ambedkar accused the Christian missionaries of being "an instrument of de-socialisation."[8] He and his followers subsequently moved into Neo-Buddhism.

In the chapter titled "Christ and the Other Faiths" in *The Christ of the Indian Road*, Jones addresses the conflict between Brahminical Hinduism and the Hindus of the lower communities. While the situation of the Dalits and the other marginalized segments were not seriously addressed about a century ago, when the book was written, with a certain degree of foresight, Jones argued that caste discrimination was alien to the core of Hinduism. As he puts it, "Some of the outward practices of Hinduism are dying, but there are behind these practices some ideas that constitute the living spirit of Hinduism

8. B. A. M. Paradkar, "The Religious Quest of Ambedkar: The Religious and Ideological Background of the Neo-Buddhist Movement among the Scheduled Castes in India," in *Ambedkar and the Neo-Buddhist Movement*, edited by T. S. Wilkinson and M. M. Thomas (Chennai: Christian Literature Society, 1972), 60.

and have made it survive through the centuries. Caste and idolatry and Brahmanism will drop away, but there will be left what will constitute the core of the Indian heritage. It will be worth preserving" (192).

Jones further points out that Jesus reconciled all human and social differences and brought them to fulfillment in him. Jesus stands between the Greeks and the Hindus, midway between East and West, and announces, "I am the Way, the Truth, and the Life" (John 14:6). Turning toward the Greeks, he says, "I am the Way"—a method of acting—the Greek's Good; "I am the Truth"—the Greek's True; "I am the Life"—the Greek's Beautiful, for Life is beauty—plus. Turning toward the Hindus he says, "I am the Way"—the Karma Marga, a method of acting; "I am the Truth"—the Gyana Marga—the method of knowing; "I am the Life"—the Bhakti Marga—the method of emotion, for Life is emotion—plus.

Conclusion

Dr. E. Stanley Jones worked and wrote with a hope to see Jesus "naturalized upon the Indian Road" (63). He would have been certain that this road would not remain a singular path but evolve with many by-lanes and crossroads, as he was aware of the diversity of cultures and religious persuasions in India. A century later, the Indian roads had become much harder and less travelled ones for Jesus because, unlike what Dr. Jones would have anticipated, there are numerous roadblocks and dead ends, not to mention the potholes on the ways and byways. From the times of Dr. Jones, the national context of India has changed beyond recognition, the contours of mission have become complicated, the inter religious conversations have become harder, lesser, and fewer. In addition, there is confusion in Christian witness coupled with a loss of credibility for the institutionalised and denominational churches in India. Thus, the challenge in presenting and witnessing to Christ has become much more challenging today than a century before.

The projects of political totalitarianism in collusion with capitalism of various avatars; cultural exclusivism in the guise of majoritarianism and/or identity affirmations; and religious nationalism subsuming all the "others" in perceptions and policymaking, in propaganda and practices make the Indian public space constricted and even threatening for the presentation of Christ. The friendly acceptance or even the hesitant welcome received by Western missionaries like Dr. Jones during the pre-independence India or in the early decades after independence had fostered great hope for Dr. Jones to believe that India had accepted Christ in spirit, both through "regular" channels like evangelistic witness and "irregular" channels like the ideals and practices of nationalist leaders like Gandhi and the various reform movements. The political and religious context of the post-independence India, especially in the last few decades, has shown an alarming decrease in tolerance on the one hand and an orchestrated move on the other to diminish even the indirect impact of Christ or Christianity in the public space and among the general public, especially at the margins of the society.

The absence of Christian leaders and church members actively involved in nation building has also contributed to the lack of Christ's presence in the public space. Dr. Jones and some Indian Christian leaders believed that "participation in the life of the nation was a way to witness Jesus."[9] The churches in India, with their inclination to an apolitical and otherworldly faith, may secure their existence to some extent against the onslaught of majoritarian and totalitarian regimes but will fail

9. M. M. Thomas, *Christian Participation in Nation-Building: The Summing up of a Corporate Study on Rapid Social Change* (Bangalore: NCCI & CISRS, 1960), iv; cf. Jones, *The Christ of the Indian Road*, "vital interest in India," 80.

to witness Jesus the crucified-risen Christ. *The Christ of the Indian Road* is a timeless call to all Christians to not shy away from the public space of India.

The contours of mission in India remain diverse and divergent, with differing modes of perceptions and practices. As in the times of Dr. Jones, one section of the churches and mission organizations tend to believe in evangelism as a means for the transformation of individuals, while another section tends to emphasize societal and structural transformation. These complementary perspectives become competing ones at times and thereby complicate the missional mode of churches. Many a time, there is confusion among the believers and leadership on what mission would mean, what the content of mission and mode of mission should be in India. Enactment of anti-conversion laws with stringent punishment adds to the fear and insecurity of those who would like to practice their Christian faith and want to present it to others.

A similar confusion can be inferred in interreligious dialogues in post-independence India. While Dr. Jones and like-minded missionaries were able to have dialogue with intellectuals and leaders, mainly of Hinduism, such dialogues have become fewer and harder now. The very purpose of interreligious dialogue has become a matter of debate for various reasons. Like for Jones, interreligious dialogue has been construed by many as a means of presenting Jesus—to win others, but not to win arguments. Jones proposed and practiced interreligious dialogue as a means of appreciating the core of Indian cultures and Hinduism to have a more enriched India with Christ. However, such a perception of interreligious dialogue has become a contested one, even among Christians. The interreligious dialogues are increasingly diminishing in India today, and the dialogue with religions other than Hinduism is hardly evident. Dialogues with even Hinduism have become a showcase event for few organisations. It is evident that interreligious dialogue in India is facing a dead end.

Another roadblock, if not a dead end, for Jesus in India is caused by the loss of credibility of Christians and churches in India. Even in the times of Dr. Jones, a general concern and critique from devout and learned people of other faiths and from national political leaders, including Mahatma Gandhi and B. R. Ambedkar, directed at Christians and churches was their apparent gap from Jesus the Christ in their lives and practices. In this sense, the values of Christians and the credibility of institutional churches had always been criticised and blamed for the lack of acceptance of Jesus on the Indian Road. While not blaming others for the criticism and while not imagining a criticism-free India, the churches, especially the institutional churches, need to ponder and reform from within by an ongoing self-examination in the "light of Jesus," scrutinizing her affairs, interdenominational relationships, internal power sharing, values, and principles. Even though Dr. Jones had deliberately avoided addressing various maladies of the India of his time, like the caste system, the churches in India can no longer mask or wish away caste and related perspectives, practices, problems, and possibilities. Churches in India often stumble upon the issue of caste, within and without.

Another task that Dr. Jones had not given much attention, deliberately though, was an Indian interpretation of Jesus Christ, a task that he "left to later hands" (63). How such an interpretation has been attempted in India in the last century is to be a lingering question for the Indian churches, theologians, thinkers, and believers in Christ in India. Even at present, Christianity is being criticised as being a "pale copy" of Western culture, the mission church, and evangelists. The experiments like the ashram movement have become stagnant, and new experiments are yet to emerge. Dr. Jones, his ashram, and his book remain an invitation for Indian Christians and churches to not copy the past or the West but to experience the person of Christ and present Christ in a plurality of forms, fonts, and soil colors of India. This remains an uncharted road for Christ.

Dr. Jones, in his proclamations or dialogues or writings, has taken great care to not deviate his attention away from the Person of Jesus, which remains a great and worthy challenge for all Christians in all contexts and all times. Bartering the Person of Jesus for his principles, or in Dr. Jones's terms, "the Whom" for "the what" (177), may make Jesus acceptable to many and profitable for the churches, but it would end up, Dr. Jones rightly cautions, as a populistic abstraction of the word from the incarnated Word. Such an attempt would be like robbing Christ from Christianity.

Presenting the person of Christ, and very pointedly the crucified Christ, is the worthy mission of any believer of Christ. This may look risky, dangerous, and life threatening. It may have no guarantee for acceptance or success. The challenge and call, however, is to remain faithful to this call and commission on the by-lanes, side-ways, and highways of India. Because of a climate of fear and hostility and for other reasons, more than at any other time in the past, today we need a contextual version of *The Christ of the Indian Road* that affirms the gospel that sheds light in the midst of gloom and darkness.

> Now the cross never knows defeat for it itself is Defeat, and you cannot defeat Defeat. You cannot break Brokenness. It starts with defeat and accepts that as a way of life. But in that very attitude it finds its victory. It never knows when it is defeated, for it turns every impediment into an instrument, and every difficulty into a door, every cross into a means of redemption. (93)

Dr. Theodosius Mar Thoma is the Metropolitan (the Supreme Head) of the Mar Thoma Syrian Church, a global church with 1.6 million members in various countries. After completing his graduate degree in science, he secured a master's degree in comparative religions from the Vishwa-Bharati University and a doctoral degree from the McMaster University. As a bishop, he served in various countries, including for seven years as the Bishop of Canada and the USA, from 2009 to 2016. He was elevated as the Supreme Head of the Mar Thoma Syrian Church in 2020. He has authored a number of books and articles.

The Christ of the Indian Road

Dr. Sathianathan Clarke

E. Stanley Jones (1884–1973) came to India as an American Methodist missionary in 1907. Among his numerous books written about living for Jesus Christ among the diverse communities in India, *The Christ of the Indian Road* (first published in 1925) was the most well-received by Christians worldwide. It sold over a million copies in the first year of its publication. As an Indian native who came to the United States twenty years ago to teach theology, mission, and world Christianity at a prominent United Methodist seminary in Washington DC (a reversal of the long-standing convention of Christian mission flowing from West to East), it is a privilege to offer this modest essay for the celebrated republication of this still edifying and engaging book.

A whole century separates a time like his from a time like ours. In 1924 (assuming E. Stanley Jones was writing this manuscript at that time for a 1925 publication), India was still under Western colonial rule. This was nothing other than the invasive expansion of British colonialism that transgressed onto an ancient Hindu-Buddhist-Jain civilization with Muslim and Sikh influences. During the colonial era (Battle of Plassey in 1757 to Indian independence in 1947), there were concerted Christian missions to destroy other religious pathways by a weighty overlay of Jesus, the Way. This was a disruptive mission model. It caused shame, hurt, and resentment that has carried over into our times. However, respectful Christian missionaries of the Good News also sat among people from various religious pathways in love and humility, offering gifts placed in their treasure chests by God. This was a "giftive mission" model.[1] It encouraged the respectful exchange of gifts and mutual transformation, a caring spirit of interreligious hospitality.

Today, in 2024 (as I write, a century after Jones penned his thoughts), India has emerged as a major economic and political player on the world stage. From an age of rebellion against foreign empires, India has consolidated its journey toward social, economic, and political freedom. Yet a change in fortunes for India as a postcolonial country has not been good news for all religious communities. Increasingly, the strong Hindu-identified nation-state has flexed its muscles to coerce and control religious minorities. Hindu nationalism spearheaded by the Bharatiya Janata Party (BJP), ideologically buttressed by the right-wing paramilitary Rashtriya Swayamsevak Sangh (RSS), is stridently and, at times, violently disrupting and squashing other ways of being religious on the fabricated hyper-religious Hindu highway. The BJP has ruled India since 2014 and has just been elected to a third five-year term, even if this time, Prime Minister Narendra Modi will govern in a coalition with other political parties. The disruptive mission of Hindu nationalism has turned against Muslims, Sikhs, and Christians, denigrating the treasured gifts bestowed upon other religions to contribute to the well-being of all Indians.

In rereading *The Christ of the Indian Road*, I was struck by traces of E. Stanley Jones's reflective and respectful pilgrimage on the multireligious pathways constituting the Indian Road. Let me point to two missionary traits that might provide hints

1. See Terry C. Muck and Frances S. Adeney, *Christianity Encountering World Religions: The Practice of Mission in the Twenty-First Century* (Grand Rapids: Baker Academic, 2009).

that Jones espoused an alternative to the colonizing propensity of Christian mission during the age of the British Empire. I think that these characteristics of mission-sans-coloniality might well be something that all religions can emulate, especially when one is the powerful ruling majority in interreligious situations. So, what are the facets of Jones's Christian mission that refused to share in colonial attitudes and practices?

Let me state the principles of colonial mission and then show how Jones refused such misinformed premises. First, colonial mission combined an uncritical attitude of veneration of the religious and cultural worldview of the missionaries with a cultivated repulsion toward the religion and culture of those they sought to missionize. Such an epistemological template viewed the relationship between the colonists and the natives to be antithetical, somewhat akin to the relationship between subjects and objects, somebodies and somethings, and those freed by the Divine and those enslaved by demons. Jones would not be molded into such a colonial binary mindset, which was blind to the failings of Christianity in the West and disrespectful to the religions and cultures of India. He confesses publicly, "Some of the contacts of the West with the East have been . . . ugly and un-Christian." He enumerates three colossal sins of Christian mission in the West. First, all of Russia was converted to Christianity by "domination" through aggressive conquering by Vladimir the Great. Second, violence was never renounced, even for the newly baptized, so war was legitimized by the expansion of Christianity. He narrates the refusal of Saxons to allow their right hand to go down into the water of baptism, to allow this hand of war to continue to kill ably even after conversion to Christianity. Third, the slave trade of Black bodies and freedom for White Christians were two sides of the same mission endeavor. "The Mayflower that carried the Pilgrim Fathers to religious liberty in America," he bemoans, "went on her next trip for a load of slaves" (72).

Apart from criticizing Christianity's destructive role in the West, Jones also lifts the positive side of Indian culture, which, in his judgment, is changing for the better. He does this by focusing on Jesus coming to the Indian masses through the "irregular channels" manifested through the work of Gandhi. In a bold statement, Jones recognizes the Spirit of Jesus overflowing onto Gandhi: "The silent pressure of the spirit of Gandhi was doing its work. And Gandhi's spirit was being pressed upon by the Spirit of Jesus" (121). From his various books, especially *Gandhi: Portrayal of a Friend* (1948), we know about Jones's deep friendship with and admiration of Mohandas Karamchand Gandhi (1869–1948). Even if Gandhi did not acknowledge Jesus as the only way to God, Jones was convinced that he walked in "the Spirit of Jesus" toward Truth, embracing nonviolence in thought, word, and action. No wonder Jones respected and learned from him while also praying that Gandhi would not only be well-versed in knowledge about Jesus but also have an intimate experience of him.

Second, colonial mission isolated individuals' beliefs and behavior from the communal solidarity and welfare of native peoples. Christian colonial mission thus focused on the personal aspects of one's faith alone. What converts believed about Christ was all it took to enter heaven. Faith affirmation or doctrinal assent was the center of mission agents as they sought to win souls for Christ. Jones may have come to India with a passion for saving individuals into eternal life in heaven. However, he soon made the kingdom of God, at hand on earth, rather than in heaven and assured in the afterlife, the center of the gospel of Jesus Christ. In a later companion to *The Christ of the India Road* titled *Along the Indian Road* (1939), Jones speaks of the "master-word" of the Christian gospel, which must no longer be hidden in seeking the welfare of India: the kingdom of God.[2]

2. E. Stanley Jones, *Along the Indian Road*, rev. ed. (Potomac, MD: E. Stanley Jones Foundation, 2022), 176.

Jones would have none of the colonial truncation of the gospel of Jesus Christ. He was a preacher of the full gospel, for this, indeed, was the teaching of his Master. In his words, "He [Jesus] proclaimed the Kingdom of God. Jesus went about 'preaching the gospel of the Kingdom.' It was the center around which everything revolved. This Kingdom seemed to be a new Order standing at the door of the lower order ready to replace it both in the individual and in the collective will with God's way of life."[3] Social holiness was intricately woven into personal piety in Jones's proclamation of the kingdom of God.

In *The Christ of the Indian Road*, Jones was already aware of the social prospect of the Christian gospel. Despite religious, gender, caste, and class differences, there was a pressing need for Indians to join in solidarity to gain their freedom from the British. The freedom and dignity of the kingdom of God were part of the good news for India. As he expounds in this book, Christ's road leads to a heaven that has landed on earth. Jesus, says Jones, "did not paint a Utopia, far off and unrealizable—he announced that the kingdom of heaven is within us, and is 'at hand' and can be realized here and now" (201). It is this social, concrete, and compassionate gospel that E. Stanley Jones emphasizes in an India that was looking for a road toward liberty, justice, and freedom. Interpreting the Last Judgment in Matthew 25:31-46, which centers on whether one evades or attends to the hungry, thirsty, sick, imprisoned, stranger, and naked in our midst, Jones insists that Christ invites those on the Indian Road to follow in a concrete, this-worldly way. Jesus, as "the Son of Fact," seeks "true followers," he says, who would be "sons of fact," since "He was not only concrete himself, he demanded a concrete life from those who were his followers" (203). The dislocation of the individual through Christian mission fragmented the solidarity of local communities. In *The*

3. Jones, *Along the Indian Road*, 79.

Christ of the Indian Road, Jones reunites colonized communities that sought the well-being of their collective life in the world with the sanctuary of distinct selves invested in securing everlasting life in God's world, gifted through Christ.

E. Stanley Jones walked by faith, in hope, and for love in the far-from-home winding roads of the Indian subcontinent. He came in sincere humility and deep respect for all God's diverse people treading the Indian Road. He desires that they would all experience Christ, who walked alongside them. Jesus journeyed through life with and for them. He did not want to get into the weeds of doctrine, creeds, and rituals to convict and judge his Indian sojourners. Jones was not an argumentative lawyer. He was a compassionate witness to the person of Jesus Christ. In this book, Jones's wisdom flows out from the compassionate heart of a passionate evangelist. I have no doubt that while reading *The Christ of the Indian Road*, you will be stirred, stretched, and schooled. But I also know you will be provoked and enriched, as I have been.

Dr. Sathianathan "Sathi" Clarke is Professor of Theology, Culture, and Mission and holds the Bishop Sundo Kim Chair in World Christianity at Wesley Theological Seminary in Washington, DC. He is also lecturer in Theology and Mission at United Theological College (Charles Sturt University) in Sydney, Australia. An ordained Presbyter of the Church of South India, he also serves as Assisting Clergy at the Church of the Epiphany, Diocese of Washington. He has worked passionately for justice with the poor and oppressed in India and elsewhere and has traveled extensively to educate and encourage interreligious dialogue. In addition to coediting several volumes, he is the author of a number of journal articles and two books: "Competing Fundamentalisms: Violent Extremism in Christianity, Islam, and Hinduism" and "Dalits and Christianity: Subaltern Religion and Liberation Theology in India."

"India Has Become Dear to Me": E. Stanley Jones's Receptive Spirit

Rev. Dr. John Thatamanil

"The Spirit of the Living Christ"

It is not often that one reads a book from 1925 and yet feels drawn into the future, the future of theology, the future of missiology, Christology, and even interreligious encounter. E. Stanley Jones's *The Christ of the Indian Road* is such a book. It is a work of theological genius, one that deserves that status of a classic and rewards constant rereading.

Urgent questions will haunt contemporary readers as they approach this text: In an era of interreligious dialogue, is there still room for talk about evangelism? If so, what form should evangelical work take? How should those who speak for Jesus and his kingdom regard the wisdom of other traditions? Must we believe that other traditions are irredeemable in order to give witness to what Christians have encountered in Jesus? With respect to these queries, it is astonishing just how much Jones gets right. E. Stanley Jones is a genuine visionary. Contemporary Christian thinkers are not nearly finished learning from him; truth be told, many of us have yet to begin.

At the heart of Jones's vision is a profound conviction that Jesus Christ is not at Christian disposal. Christ is already at work in the encounter between traditions in ways that we can neither anticipate nor control. The Christian task is to *follow* the living Christ who walks along the Indian Road and always remains ahead of us. Jones believes that evangelists must follow what Christ is always already doing in the world rather than strive to bring Christ to a Christ-forsaken world. This call remains as urgent now as when it was first sounded.

Still, we must not tell a Pollyannaish tale. Ours is a dire time in which the rightward turn advanced by militant Hindutva and its majoritarian attack on Muslims and on Christians—recall for example, the horrific murder of Graham Staines and his sons—raise dire questions about the viability and even rightness of the evangelical task. Is there still room for evangelical witness in India when relations between traditions have become so intensely fraught? Does Jones still have anything to teach us in this moment of political and intercommunal crises? Can we still read Jones productively when Nathuram Godse—Gandhi's assassin—not Gandhi himself is in the ascendancy on the Indian scene? These questions must be confronted as we reckon with Jones's book. Jones cannot offer us all the answers we need for a time that he could not have envisioned, but his book remains a generative resource, a companion in the life of faith that must not be left neglected on the dust-covered shelves of the historical past.

The central task of Jones's book is to inform readers that a vast spiritual movement is taking place in India. Christ is being rediscovered afresh in a distinctively Indian key. Long before Christian theologians began talking about "indigenization" or "contextualization," Jones was already sounding these themes, albeit without access to these terms. Jones's farsighted genius in this respect is striking. Every people and every nation, Jones contends, must discover the meaning of Christ and his gospel anew from the perspective of their *distinctive* national and cultural intuitions. Jones writes,

> The religious genius of India is the richest in the world, the forms that it has taken have often been the most extravagant, sometimes degrading and cruel. These forms are falling away, or will fall away, but the spirit persists and will be poured through other forms. As that genius pours itself through Christian molds it will enrich the collective expression of Christianity. But in order to do that the Indian must remain Indian. He must stand in the stream of India's culture and life and let the force of that stream go through his soul so that the expression of Indian Christianity will be essentially Eastern and not Western. This does not mean that Indian Christianity will be denied what is best in Western thought and life, for when firmly planted on its own soil it can then lift its antennae to the heavens and catch the voices of the world. But it must be particular before it can be universal. Only thus will it be creative—a voice, not an echo. (208)

No progressive contemporary reader will respond warmly to talk that depicts forms of Indian religious life as "sometimes degrading and cruel." Jones cannot be swallowed whole, and discernment is necessary. But such moments of critique mark a minor note in *The Christ of the Indian Road*. In fact, in Jones's "Preface to the Sixth Edition," he tells us that he has fielded critique from Christian contemporaries for his omission in this book of the negative features of Indian religious life. As to the reasons for this omission, Jones responds,

> India is aggrieved, and I think rightly so, that Christian missionaries in order to arouse the West to missionary activity have too often emphasized the dark side of the picture. What they have said has been true, but the picture has not been a true one. This overemphasis on

> the one side has often created either pity or contempt in the minds of the hearers. In modern jargon a superiority complex has resulted. (65)

Readers can bear Jones's indictment because he offers stark words after a genuine and long intimacy with Indian religious communities. Although Jones speaks in this book of his calling to engage the cultural life of high-caste Hindus ("gone only to" 76)—a calling that he regards as imposed upon him rather than voluntarily undertaken—he is nonetheless unsparing about how caste distorts all of Indian life. Crucially, being engaged with reform-minded Indians, Jones's critiques are never stones thrown from outside the house but are derived from within the Hindu household. In almost all cases, words of critique within this book come from Hindu reformers themselves and not simply from Jones's foreign perspective as an American missionary. We might well have reservations about such critiques, but what is striking—given the time—is all that he has to say positively about India's exalted religious heritage.

By way of striking contrast, recall Macaulay's infamous "Minute on Indian Education," where he entertains a rather different hope for at least one segment of the Indian elite: "We must at present do our best to form a class who may be interpreters between us and the millions whom we govern—a class of persons Indian in blood and colour, but English in tastes, in opinions, in morals and in intellect."[1] Macaulay exhibits the pernicious chauvinism that Jones names as one of the great "hindrances" to effective Christian witness in India. Jones, by contrast, insists that "the Indian must remain Indian."

The Indian must remain Indian not only for the Indian's own sake but also to advance the fortunes of the gospel. Only when the gospel is heard and then interpreted in a genuinely

1. T. B. Macauly, "Minute on Education," February 2, 1835, https://home.iitk.ac.in/~hcverma/Article/Macaulay-Minutes.pdf.

Indian key will we come to a new understanding of who Christ is and may yet be. Christ may well be "the same yesterday and today and forever," (Hebrews 13:8). Still, Jones proclaims a living Christ, a living and acting Christ who is yet becoming and unfolding within the distinctive national and cultural contexts in which he is encountered. If those particular contexts are erased, if missionaries preach a colonizer's gospel that erases what is distinctive about Indian cultural life, then the pernicious result would be a sickly Western Christianity transplanted into Eastern soil producing only a short-lived echo rather than a distinctive voice. Jones insists that only a Christ of the Indian Road can give life to India.

Does talk of Christ of the Indian Road mean that Jones means to offer us a genuinely Indian Christology? Jones is, from the first, aware that this cannot be his task. He insists that his task is not to produce "an Indian interpretation of Christ. It is, rather, an attempt to describe how Christ is becoming naturalized upon the Indian Road. The Indian interpretation of Christ must be left to later hands" (63). Jones's judiciousness and humility in circumscribing the work that is fitting for him is remarkable, and the language of naturalization is fecund and arresting. He takes himself to be a humble listener who discerns incipient trends rather than as one who presumes to prescribe to Indians what form Indian Christologies ought to take. Nonetheless, a careful reading of this book will demonstrate that Jones hears and describes well the Christ who is emerging in what the Mar Thoma theologian M. M. Thomas would much later (1969) describe as *The Acknowledged Christ of the Indian Renaissance*.[2]

What is most remarkable about the Christological notes that Jones sounds is that *The Christ of the Indian Road*

2. M. M. Thomas, *The Acknowledged Christ of the Indian Renaissance* (London: SCM Press, 1969).

explicitly repudiates the wholesale rejection of other traditions. For Jones, proclaiming Christ in no way demands a rejection of the deep spirit of Hindu traditions. On this point, Jones is emphatic. So convincing and farsighted is Jones in this respect that we have not yet begun to equal his distinctive mode of evangelical witness. Moreover, Jones is clear that he comes to India to commend Christ, not to commend Christianity, let alone an imported Western Christianity that has to be accepted in total. What a genuinely Indian Christianity will become, Jones insists, cannot yet be specified. As already stated, that is a work to be left between the Christ of the Indian Road and the open hearts who receive him. Jones is even open to the possibility that those who receive the Christ might yet and still wish to remain outside of Christianity. But that, Jones insists, is not the evangelist's business. His task is only to commend the Christ, who always goes before him.

E. Stanley Jones and Mohandas Gandhi: On Receiving the Wisdom India Has to Give

To spell out what I mean, I want to begin by noting the second central character in Jones's book: Mohandas Gandhi. A word search for "Gandhi" finds 63 mentions.[3] For the sake of comparison, the term "kingdom" occurs only 29 times, and Christ, of course, 267 times. It should go without saying that Christ is the central character of Jones's book. Numerical data can only tell us so much, but numbers are telling nonetheless. Jones explicitly and repeatedly acknowledges that the fortunes of Christ on the Indian Road depend considerably on the

3. I am including in this count two infelicitous misspellings of his name as "Ghandi."

Mahatma. For Jones, Gandhi's contribution is critical, and to this theme we will return.

But I appeal to Gandhi here in order to affirm that E. Stanley Jones is among the few distinguished missionaries to India who exemplified the virtues that Gandhi himself commended to missionaries. In other writing, I have observed that Gandhi was routinely invited to address gatherings of Christian missionaries. Fascinated both by his evident love for Jesus but his adamant refusal to convert, Gandhi presented an intriguing puzzle for Christian missionaries. In return, Gandhi sounded a recurring theme that I have called "the hospitality of receiving." The term is mine but the notion is most definitely Gandhi's. It is important to hear Gandhi in his own words:

> I place these facts before you in all humility for the simple reason that you may know this land better, the land to which you have come to serve. You are here to find out the distress of the people of India and remove it. But I hope you are here also in a receptive mood, and if there is anything that India has to give, you will not stop your ears, you will not close your eyes, and steel your hearts, but open up your ears, eyes, and most of all your hearts to receive all that may be good in this land. I give you my assurance that there is a great deal of good in India. Do not flatter yourselves with the belief that a mere recital of that celebrated verse in St. John makes a man a Christian. If I have read the Bible correctly, I know many men who have never heard the name of Jesus Christ or have even rejected the official interpretation of Christianity who will, probably, if Jesus came in our midst today in the flesh, be owned by him more than many of us. I therefore ask you to approach the problem before you with openheartedness and humility.[4]

---

4. Mohandas Gandhi, *Gandhi on Christianity*, ed. Robert Ellsberg (Maryknoll, NY: Orbis Books), 40, Kindle.

Gandhi's appeal to missionaries is poignant. He rightly believed—as did Jones—that regnant missionary attitudes towards India were marked by condescension and, as Jones put it, a "superiority complex." Against this elitist posture, Gandhi invites missionaries to come to India with open hands and open hearts. To missionaries he says to be prepared to receive not merely to give. In fact, Gandhi makes the logic of his plea explicit when he states,

> The powers of God should not be limited by the limitations of our understanding. To you who have come to teach India, I therefore say, you cannot give without taking. If you have come to give rich treasures of experiences, open your hearts out to receive the treasures of this land, and you will not be disappointed, neither will you have misread the message of the Bible.[5]

Gandhi is clear. If missionaries maintain a posture in which they come to India only to give but maintain that they have nothing to receive in return, they will do neither. Instead, they will only manage to wound. Missionaries must undergo a conversion of the heart and enter into a "receptive mood." It is not too much to say that Gandhi holds out expectation that the religious history of humankind itself might enter into a new era in which traditions might be enriched by what the great Spanish-Indian theologian Raimon Panikkar would much later call their "mutual fecundation." Through the giving and receiving of their distinctive gifts and charisms, a deeper wisdom can emerge that no religious tradition could have anticipated in isolation.

Indeed, Gandhi suspects that such mutual giving and receiving will lead to new readings of each tradition's scriptures. The Bible's exclusive verses—he mentions in particular

5. Gandhi, *Gandhi on Christianity*, 41–42.

the Gospel of John—will receive a new hearing and new spiritual import when traditions move into genuine encounter. When persons from different religious traditions meet in this spirit, Gandhi holds that dramatically new possibilities in the religious unfolding of humankind will emerge: "If we were to put the spiritual experiences together, we would find a resultant which would answer the cravings of human nature."[6] A dramatic and even visionary possibility—a possibility to which, I believe, Jones remains remarkably open.

Why so much about Gandhi within an essay on E. Stanley Jones? Well, as I have already noted, Gandhi is a pivotal, indeed central, figure in Jones's book. Jones observes that the emergence of a genuinely Indian Christianity is taking place precisely through Gandhi's leadership. It is Gandhi's reception of Jesus that is opening Indian hearts to the Christ of the Indian Road.

But my primary reason for this extended engagement with Gandhi is that few Christian missionaries or theologians—and I count Jones a distinguished theologian indeed—have so fully answered Gandhi's call for an openhearted and humble receptivity to what India has to give than E. Stanley Jones. So, what is it in particular that Jones believes that Christians have to learn from India. Here, it is imperative to quote him at some length. From India, Jones believes that there are "five living seeds" to be received:

> (1) That the ultimate reality is spirit. (2) The sense of unity running through things. (3) That there is justice at the heart of the universe. (4) A passion for freedom. (5) The tremendous cost of the religious life. I do not believe that the world can afford to lose those five things so deeply imbedded in India's thought and life. (192)

6. Gandhi, *Gandhi on Christianity*, 41.

I do not intend to go through what Jones means by treating each of these enumerated items. I wish only to note the profundity of Jones's enumeration. He is explicitly accepting Gandhi's challenge to missionaries that they must be prepared to *receive* from India's spiritual treasury. Jones answers Gandhi's call not with vague generalities but with theological specificity. The themes that Jones enumerates here, particularly the first two, point to the nondualism of Advaita Vedanta. There is but one undergirding reality. It is, in the classical terms of Sri Shankaracarya, being (*sat*), consciousness (*cit*), and infinity (*ananta*). It is the self of the self (*atman*), or Spirit. These are permanent gifts to the religious heritage of humankind.

In our day, this work of learning from and with other traditions is called "comparative theology." Comparative theologians insist that real interreligious learning is possible across traditions. The beginnings of the field in its contemporary iteration date back to the work of Francis X. Clooney, SJ, Robert C. Neville, Keith Ward, and Raimon Panikkar, who began to write actively as comparative theologians only in the 1980s. By contrast, Jones begins to do the work of comparative theology a full sixty years before these groundbreaking figures! Note also that Jones is arguing that it is "the world" that cannot afford to lose India's distinctive religious genius. The stakes are enormous. Like Gandhi, Jones believed that the spiritual heritage of humankind itself is at stake in the encounter between traditions.

Contemporary comparative theologians tend not to speak in such global terms, nor would they risk essentializing "India" as a whole. These cautionary notes notwithstanding, we must recognize that Jones is insisting that Indic religious traditions have indispensable gifts that cannot be lost. He comes to India with an open hand and not as one who comes only to give and not to receive. Indeed, he tells us as much. Let us hear his poignant confessional words about how India has converted him. Jones writes:

> India has become very dear to me. But I find that my love for India has a quality in it now that it did not have in the early days. I went to India through pity, I stay through respect. I love India because she is lovable, I respect her because she is respectable; she has become dear to me because she is endearing. (222)

One can only wonder what shape Indian national life would have taken if more missionaries to India had adopted Jones's receptive and respectful spirit.

"India Is Aggrieved" Redux: India Between Violence and Nonviolence

We have already mentioned that Jones begins his book with his observation that "India is aggrieved." That perceptive comment notwithstanding, he could hardly have anticipated how this aggrievement would subsequently unfold. Jones is alert to the ever-present possibility of violence stirring in India's independence struggles. Still, the events that led up to and following the destruction of the Babri Masjid (December 6, 1992) could not have been anticipated by even the keenest of prophets.

In one of the great ironies of history, Jones's irenic and optimistic book was published the very year that the militant organization Rashtra Swayamsevak Sangh was founded.[7] Indeed, two years before the publication of Jones's book, V. D. Savarkar coined the term "Hindutva" (1923), which has come to define the Indian scene far more comprehensively than the term "Hinduism." Unsurprisingly, neither Savarkar's name nor

7. See Subhasree Chakravarty, "'A Majority with a Minority Complex': Reorientation of Myths and the Making of Hindu Cadres," *South Asian Review* 45, no. 3 (2023).

his then newly minted term occurs within the pages of *The Christ of the Indian Road*.

But it must be observed that Gandhi is already named a "failure" in this book, albeit a great and inspiring failure. The reasons for this reckoning would be well known to any student of India's history in the early 1920s. Gandhi, after his return to India from South Africa (1915), assumed leadership of the Indian National Congress and the Indian Noncooperation Movement. After notable early success, Gandhi felt compelled to call off his civil disobedience campaign after the events that took place on February 4, 1922, in the village of Chauri Chaura, events in which mob violence led to the killing of twenty-two policemen. The eruption of violence in the nonviolence movement that Gandhi led was a bitter disappointment to the Mahatma and led to his suspension of any further collective action. This is the moment of disruption and disappointment in which Jones writes:

> Gandhi did not fail. The Indian people failed Gandhi. It was their failure. But in apparent failure he really succeeded. I would rather think of him as Gandhi the defeated, but holding firm and with fresh spirit to the belief that somehow, someway the power of his ideal must conquer, than to see Gandhi seated by some other method as the first president of the Indian Republic. (116)

Notwithstanding the power of these lines, they pale in comparison to those in which Jones compares Gandhi to Jesus himself. When confronted by skeptics as to why Gandhi's name is so routinely on Jones's lips despite the failure of his movement, he writes, "I replied that I did so because I belonged to that other and greater Failure of human history—to the Man who began a kingdom with initial success and then it all ended in a cross, a bitter and shameful Failure. But Golgotha's failure was the world's most amazing success" (115). It is quite remarkable indeed that Jones is prepared to so directly compare Jesus's crucifixion—his defeat—with Gandhi's own defeat. Critical to this comparison is that, ultimately, neither defeat proves to be final.

Failing to recognize that *The Christ of the Indian Road* is written in the immediate aftermath of Chauri Chaura, Gandhi's imprisonment, the fracturing of the Indian National Congress and prior to the remarkable events yet to unfold in the march toward Indian independence would be to badly misread the living context in which this book emerges. But, having already spoken about Jones and Gandhi at some length above, I return to him here only to note that the birth of this book took place at a critical juncture in which violence rather than nonviolence appeared to have ascendancy. Nevertheless, Jones's mood was one of optimism. Jones regarded Gandhi's campaign of nonviolence as the most radical and efficacious introduction of meaning of the cross into the Indian imagination.

If in this book, Stanley Jones could not have guessed at the dramatic Gandhi-led events that would soon unfold over the course of the following two decades, events culminating in India's independence, how could he have guessed the radical overturning of the Gandhian legacy in India that we are now living through? Arguably, the claim that "The Indian people have failed Gandhi" is more on target now than it was in 1925. Hindutva majoritarianism explicitly cultivates and then wields aggrievement as a political wedge tool to mobilize Hindu majorities against India's religious minorities, Muslims most of all.

Further complicating the contemporary scene are the ongoing attacks on the possibility of conversion. E. Stanley Jones, by contrast, writes rapturously about the quickening impulse of Gandhi's self-imposed twenty-one-day fast in the wake of intercommunal violence. Here's Jones:

> But the most remarkable resolution was the one in which they stated that "We recognize the right of an individual to change his faith at will, provided no inducement is offered to effect that change, such as the offering of material gain," and, further, "We also recognize the right of that individual not to suffer persecution from the community which he may leave." When one remembers that in Islam apostasy meant death, and in Hinduism social death, then this resolution marks a national epoch and is really a National Declaration of Religious Freedom. The silent pressure of the spirit of Gandhi was doing its work. And Gandhi's spirit was being pressed upon by the Spirit of Jesus. (121)

A "National Declaration of Religious Freedom!" It is impossible to miss Jones's joy at this turn of events. Tragically, observers of the contemporary Indian scene know all too well that this freedom to convert has been explicitly under attack in India now for some decades. The United States Commission on International Religious Freedom observes in a recent report (2023) that "twelve states in India have legislation criminalizing religious conversions in various circumstances." The report sets out to examine "the common features of India's state-level anti-conversion laws and explains why those common features are inconsistent with freedom of religion or belief under international human rights law."[8] Such laws are also arguably in violation of the Indian Constitution.[9]

---

8. See Luke Wilson, *Issue Update: India's State-Level Anti-Conversion Laws* (United States Commission on International Religious Freedom, 2023). https://www.uscirf.gov/sites/default/files/2023%20India%20Apostasy%20Issue%20Update.pdf

9. Article 19, Clause 1 of the Draft Constitution of India (1948) reads, "(1) Subject to public order, morality and health and to the other provisions of this Part, all persons are equally entitled to freedom of conscience and the right freely to profess, practise and propagate religion." The key word here, of course, is "propagate." This language remains in the present Indian Constitution in Article 25.

What are we to make of this turn of events? How do we read *The Christ of the Indian Road* in light of this dramatic shift away not only from Gandhian nonviolence but also from India's constitutionally enshrined right to "propagate religion?"[10] There are no easy answers. The present moment is one of crisis and retrenchment, of colonial blowback. The great hindrances to Christian witness that Jones mapped so well and his description of a colonial superiority complex have exacted their toll. Over the last four decades in particular, proponents of Hindutva have transformed aggrievement into a cottage industry. The result has been the creation of a "majority with a minority complex." If Hindus are the aggrieved "minority," Muslims and Christians are figured as colonizing others who must be resisted along with their traditions. The inclusion of these "others" within the Indian polity is, at best, conditional; the other's presence within the nation depends on their concession to recognize Bharat as a Hindu nation.

Under these conditions, the very possibility of Christian witness is gravely imperiled. E. Stanley Jones's gentle and winsome witness, a witness that "introduces" the Christ and leaves the question of baptism and church membership open—even this kind of witness to Christ is risky at best, if not downright dangerous at worst. At present, in the wave after wave of church destructions and other attacks on Christians, the question no longer is how Indian Christians can defend the freedom to propagate their faith but how Christians can secure their very existence.

Very recently (February 2024), the Catholic Bishops' Conference of India released a report in which they state,

10. It must, of course, be acknowledged that Gandhi was himself no fan of conversion. A full treatment of the reasons for his reluctance on this score would take us far from the work of E. Stanley Jones. Suffice it to say here that Gandhi himself had to be persuaded that freedom of religion must include the freedom to propagate one's religion.

"Attacks on Christians continue to increase in different parts of India. Destruction of homes and churches, harassment of personnel serving in orphanages, hostels, educational and healthcare institutions on false allegations of conversion have become common."[11] Conversion has become a cudgel used to justify violence. The current situation leaves missiologists in a predicament. Even Jones's approach of witnessing to Christ within a context of deep appreciation for Hindu wisdom seems a precarious strategy, one that may even risk lives. So, what are Christians to do?

In this context of suspicion, mistrust, and violence, what we can carry forward from Jones is precisely his profound capacity to *receive wisdom* from Indian religious traditions and Hinduism in particular. What we most need in this moment is a respectful and appreciative engagement with *Hinduism*, not *Hindutva*. The fortunes of Hindutva will depend on considerable measure on whether an authentic and compassionate Hinduism emerges that is strong enough to resist the depredations of Hindutva. Christians or Muslims will not save Hindus from Hindutva; only Hindus can accomplish that. The role of Christians in this context will be to embody the best of E. Stanley Jones's respectful, appreciative, and generous engagement with Hindu wisdom. Only appreciation, respect, and love will have any chance of countering aggrievement.

A Concluding Note: E. Stanley Jones as Prophet and Theologian

So much more could be said here about the treasures contained in *The Christ of the Indian Road* and what we have yet to learn from E. Stanley Jones. Consider, for example, the global

11. See Luke Coppen, "India's Bishops: 'Attacks on Christians now Common,'" *The Pillar*, February 7, 2024, https://www.pillarcatholic.com/p/indias-bishops-attacks-on-christians.

imagination of this book. Jones demonstrates an uncanny prescience about how Christians now live in global times; hence, he knows all too well that evil done by Christians in the US impedes missionary work in India. Writing as an Indian Christian immigrant in the United States, it is astonishing to read Jones's condemnation of the various Asian exclusion acts ("Immigration Law" 141-42) then being implemented in the US and how the white supremacy that undergirds these acts is impeding missionary work in India ("broken our" 145)!

Jones asks forthrightly how Christian missionaries can claim to critique India when white American Christians pass such legislation back at home. Jones is critiquing legislation that would not be repealed until the Immigration and Nationality Act of 1965, signed in the midst of the Black Freedom Movement and the Cold War. But here is a man who knows that there can be no criticism of caste in India without a criticism of race in America! I know of no comparable figure in the 1920s capable of such ethical rigor, transparency, global accountability and farsightedness, other than the black sociologist W. E. B. DuBois. A careful reading of this book will reveal that Jones routinely sounds anti-racist, anti-casteist, anti-colonial, and even anti-capitalist notes. What criticism is offered of India is more than equaled by his critique of "Western civilization" and its pretenses.

Consider also Jones's theological perspicacity and creativity. Over the last several decades, mostly at the creative impulse of process theology, the term "panentheism" has taken root in contemporary theological discourse. The invention of the term dates back to the work of the nineteenth-century German philosopher K. C. F. Krause, but its traction in contemporary theology is owed to the mid to late twentieth-century work of Charles Hartshorne and his followers.[12] But, here, quite unex-

12. See Benedikt Paul Göcke and Swami Medhananda, "Introduction" *in Panentheism in Indian and Western Thought: Cosmopolitan Interventions*, edited by Benedikt

pectedly in 1925, we see E. Stanley Jones deploying the term with great care and precision:

> Again, is it worthwhile to preserve that sense of the unity of things? India has gone too far and has slipped into pantheism—everything God—but that will be corrected to a panentheism—everything in God. This will bring us a sense of the unity of all life. It should make a more friendly and meaningful and kindly universe. (192)

I hypothesize that this must be one of the earliest usages of the term by an American theologian. It can hardly be expected that the deployment of this then abstruse term taken from German philosophy would occur in a book written by an American evangelist speaking about Indian religious life. Jones is full of surprises! Indeed, in his willingness to receive, albeit with what he believes to be needed gentle correction, Indian accounts of divine immanence, there is even the hint of what we need today for ecological awareness, namely, a "friendly and meaningful and kindly universe," one worth caring for rather than escaping from.

In these brief remarks, I hope to have persuaded readers that in just over two-hundred pages, E. Stanley Jones has managed to write what must be regarded as one of the classics of twentieth century Christian reflection. It is my earnest hope that this new edition will bring new generations of theological students and general readers to this towering work of American evangelical theology. We need Jones's vision and wisdom now more than ever.

Paul Göcke and Swami Medhananda (New York: Routledge, 2024), 1.

The Rev. Dr. John J. Thatamanil is a scholar and professor known for his work in the fields of theology, comparative theology, and interreligious dialogue. Thatamanil is Professor of Theology and World Religions at Union Theological Seminary in New York City. He is the author of the books "The Immanent Divine: God, Creation, and the Human Predicament" and, most recently, "Circling the Elephant: A Comparative Theology of Religious Diversity." He is also a priest in and diocesan theologian for the Anglican Diocese of Islands and Inlets. He serves as an associate priest both in the Anglican Church of St. John the Divine (Victoria, BC) and St. Mark's Church-in-the-Bowery (Manhattan).

My Life's Work: Knowing the Jesus That E. Stanley Jones Preached

Very Rev. Abraham O. Kadavil Corepiscopos

I know that my parents dedicated me at birth to be a priest, and that was not surprising, as our Kadavil family has a history of famous bishops among our relatives. I therefore began early to train to become a priest. I attended a parish school where I was deeply influenced by a monk [Ramban Pathros] of the Syrian Orthodox church, a person with deep convictions of fairness and justice. Father Pathros's ministry involved engaging with the low-caste people in our community, who at that time were not welcomed by the church. He founded an organization, Servants of the Cross, which I later joined and spent considerable time supporting.

Father Pathros later asked if I wished to attend Leonard Theological Seminary [LTS] in Jabalpur, in the Indian state of Madhya Pradesh. I was so pleased to attend that seminary and then discovered that I was given a scholarship supported by E. Stanley Jones. One day, Dr. Jones visited the seminary and met with a group of students. I told Dr. Jones that I had listened to him when he preached at the Maramon Convention some years before and that now I was so pleased to be able to hear him again and to speak to him in English, which I had now mastered. I also thanked him for his very generous scholarship! During ESJ's visit to LTS and Jabalpur, now a large city of over one million, he spoke to a large gathering of non-Christians. It was ESJ's habit to offer lectures to the intelligentsia of India. It seemed to me to be a potentially challenging meeting, as I did not know how the Hindu leaders would receive his message. ESJ presented Christ as the representative of God who offers salvation. He did not criticize the Hindu religion, and I found this to be a new and immensely helpful approach in the field of evangelism. I see that presentation of Christ so beautifully illustrated in his first book, *The Christ of the Indian Road*.

Sadly, that was the last time that I spent precious time with ESJ. And now I want to reflect on this question, How did E. Stanley Jones help me to be where I am today? Let me craft an answer to that question as I share information about my ministry—a ministry that has included significant educational opportunities for which I am grateful and in particular to E. Stanley Jones, who helped launch my ministry with his scholarship to LTS.

After I graduated from LTS, I received a scholarship from the World Council of Churches to attend their Ecumenical Institute at Château de Bossey in Switzerland. While residing there, I was able to attend courses about the ecumenical movement and intercultural Bible studies. I participated in several visits along with members of the Swiss Reformed Church while in Bossey, and I had the honor of visiting Emil Brunner and other well-known scholars and theologians.

I was eager for these cross-cultural experiences, perhaps in part because of ESJ's deep interest in understanding various cultural perspectives about Jesus. For example, ESJ would say that he did not bring Jesus to India, but that Jesus was already there. He wrote in *The Christ of the Indian Road*,

> The religious genius of India is the richest in the world. As that genius pours itself through Christian molds, it will enrich the collective expression of Christianity. But in order to do that the Indian must remain Indian. The Indian must stand in the stream of India's culture and life and let the force of that stream go through his soul so that the expression of Indian Christianity will be essentially Eastern and not Western. (208)

Like Jones, in my engagement with other cultures I was always looking for transferable concepts, transcultural images, and analogies relevant in other cultures that could help me communicate Jesus more convincingly in each cultural setting. Jesus is indigenous in all countries and cultures. I wanted to experience Jesus everywhere.

After this experience in Switzerland, I was invited to England, where I received another generous scholarship to study in the St. Augustine's Anglican College in Canterbury. I have always enjoyed meeting people from different parts of the world, and my study in different countries offered me a significant opportunity to get to know a wide range of wonderful people. I was eager to find a mentor knowledgeable about Eastern Orthodox theology, and an Anglican pastor, Father George Avery, a scholar in Orthodox theology, emerged as my mentor. He was a great blessing to me as I probed the depths of our Orthodox history and theology. I then got an opportunity through the Lutheran Church to go to Germany for work as a student chaplain. Here I had the opportunity to visit Pastor Martin Neimöller. I was immensely blessed, as noted above, by these cross-cultural educational experiences. However, before planning my return to my homeland, I wanted to visit the Vatican. I had the good fortune to meet Archbishop Johannes Willebrands, who was central to the increased ecumenism of the Roman Catholic Church. The archbishop told me, "When you visit Rome, please be my guest at the Vatican." I could not say no and so was welcomed by his Grace and was able to visit the Sistine Chapel and attend a Mass with the Pope. While exploring Nero's gardens in the Vatican, I met several nuns from Kerala. As they knew that I would soon be returning to India, they prevailed upon me to contact their families. I promised to do my best and followed through on my promise by contacting some of them.

Visiting the Coliseum during my time in Rome was a very moving experience. I realized that I was standing in the Coliseum, where Saint Ignatius, the patriarch of the Syriac Orthodox Church, was martyred. When Saint Ignatius refused to worship Caesar, he was taken prisoner and transferred to Rome for the emperor's spectacle as a victim thrown into the colosseum to be eaten by lions. Thus, Saint Ignatius's life was offered as a Eucharist for Christ Jesus, and for me to stand in that place was an immensely powerful experience. After visiting the Vatican, I also visited Greece as the guest of the Greek Orthodox Church.

Finally, I returned to India, where I was asked to be the general secretary of the Mar Gregorios Orthodox Christian Student Movement's (MGOCSM's) sixtieth anniversary jubilee. This wonderful organization is the oldest Christian student organization in Asia. My previous experiences in Europe working with student organizations contributed to my desire to create a center in India designed specifically to engage students, deepen their spiritual life, and foster a deep sense of fellowship. Such a center was established as the Sixtieth Anniversary Jubilee Memorial of the MGOCSM, with some financial aid from the World Council of Churches.

At this same time, I received an invitation and a scholarship to come to the Crozer Theological Seminary in the United States for further theological study. After I received my MTh degree in the US, I considered returning to India, but just then, I was asked to consider working as a hospital chaplain and obtain training in pastoral counseling. Thus, I became a chaplain at North Carolina Baptist Hospital in Winston Salem, North Carolina, and at the Vanderbilt University Medical Center in Nashville, Tennessee. Later, I moved to the Baltimore, Maryland, area to serve as a hospital chaplain at the Spring Grove Psychiatric Hospital. At that point, I was faced with a decision of whether I should remain a chaplain, where the compensation was guaranteed, or venture out as a counselor and build my own practice among faith-based organizations. I said yes to the adventure of serving as a marriage and family counselor and did so for thirty-two years. When I think back about all that went into that decision, I am reminded of my early ministry with the low-caste persons in India and the stigma associated with them. It is not that different for individuals with mental illness, who are also stigmatized. Those who suffer from such illness often live in the shadows of their communities.

Most importantly, as I reflect on my over thirty years' ministry in the field of mental health, I think again of ESJ, for I later learned about the deep interest he also had in mental health. His story is well worth retelling. After several years in India, ESJ began to experience a series of what were described as mental breakdowns. ESJ writes, "My body did not throw off disease as before and I began to have nervous collapses."[1] He was ordered to go to America on furlough to regain his shattered emotional health. He would later acknowledge that he was experiencing inner conflicts and was living and preaching beyond his experience. However, upon his return to India in 1917, the physical complaints continued, and Jones felt that he was finally unable to carry on. He believed that he was

1. E. Stanley Jones, *A Song of Ascents: A Spiritual Autobiography* (Nashville: Abingdon Press, 1968), 86.

done for, but Jesus had another plan for ESJ. During a time of prayer, ESJ gave up his shattered health to Christ and surrendered everything to God, and he was healed. Once he surrendered his all to Christ, ESJ had the full resources of Jesus available to him.

So, my brother in Christ E. Stanley Jones did know much about human suffering through his own emotional health challenges. I can relate to his experience, as I have worked closely with several people faced with such challenges. ESJ's experiences inspired one of them to take up the cause of persons with emotional illness and their families. He envisioned a place in India where people with emotional and mental health needs could find treatment in a holistic setting that addressed mind, body, and spirit. In the 1940s ESJ met frequently with Dr. Karl Menninger, the world-famous psychoanalyst, who agreed to help him establish a psychiatric center in Lucknow, India. It is the Nur Manzil (Palace of Light) Psychiatric Centre, which officially opened on December 13, 1950. It is a holistic setting that addresses mind, body, and spirit.

I understand that Nur Manzil continues to provide quality mental health care to persons from all over the Indian subcontinent. Nur Manzil is a learning and training hospital where renowned mental health professionals from the world over practice their art. Today, Nur Manzil continues to remain a pioneer in the field of psychiatry and a charitable institution offering its unique services to society at large without any discrimination because of religion, gender, social or economic status.

My gratitude for the life and ministry of E. Stanley Jones is great. I am now in my ninety-first year and continue to serve our Lord as a senior priest of the Syriac Orthodox Church.

Very Rev. Abraham O. Kadavil Corepiscopos (Father Abraham) grew up with a great familiarity with the Maramon Convention.

The Maramon Convention is an annual Christian meeting held on the vast sandy banks of the Pampa River, next to the Kozhencherry Bridge, at Maramon in Kerala, India. It is organized by the Mar Thoma Evangelistic Association, the missionary wing of the Malankara Mar Thoma Syrian Church. His mother's side of the family were Mar Thoma Church members, and his father's side of the family were members of the Syrian Orthodox Church. As he spent a good deal of time with his mother's family, he had the opportunity to attend the Maramon Convention several times. On one occasion, when he was about fourteen years old, he heard E. Stanley Jones preach at the convention, but he was so far in the back of the crowded audience that he did not see him. The next day, he decided that he wanted to see Dr. Jones preach, rather than just hear him. He left for the Maramon Convention early in the day and walked the distance to the convention site to attend a Bible study in the morning session that was delivered by Jones. Jones spoke in English. As the young boy Abraham had not yet mastered English, he depended on listening to the interpreter translate Jones's words into Malayalam. As he later reflected, "My first experience with ESJ was memorable, and little did I know that I would find my life's work in theology and knowing the Jesus that Jones preached about so eloquently." This is an edited transcript of an interview with Father Abraham and the editors on February 2, 2024.

EXPLORING THE MISSIONAL THEOLOGY OF E. STANLEY JONES AS ARTICULATED IN *THE CHRIST OF THE INDIAN ROAD*, WITH IMPLICATIONS FOR CHRISTIAN WITNESS IN THE CONTEMPORARY WORLD

Rev. Dr. Shivraj K. Mahendra

Introduction

> Jesus walks along the roads of India's thought and life and everywhere there is a new sense of values, a new feeling that there is healing in the air, a new sense that there is a springtime of the soul upon us as the old forms of life break up and melt and there are stirrings of new life all around, a new hope—a regenerating Presence has come.
>
> —E. Stanley Jones, *The Christ of the Indian Road*

Dr. E. Stanley Jones witnessed to the presence of Christ on the Indian Road. Jones knew that he did not bring Christ to India, but that Christ was already there. Jones walked on that Indian Road with his Lord and Master. During one of my walks along an Indian Road, I was introduced to E. Stanley Jones. It was the summer of 2010.[1] I met Ms. Lillian Wallace at her home in Mehragaon near the Sat Tal Christian Ashram in Uttarakhand, North India. The occasion was during my field research trip to gather information for a book on Christianity in Uttarakhand.[2] That day a seed was sown in my heart to know more about Dr. Jones and his legacy. This seed began to grow when I began to explore the missional theology of E. Stanley Jones while pursuing my PhD at Asbury Theological Seminary in the United States.

During the research, I was delighted to connect with Dr. Jones's granddaughter, Dr. Anne Mathews-Younes, the president of the E. Stanley Jones Foundation. Anne has been a great friend since then, and I have enjoyed working with her on designing, editing, and reprinting the E. Stanley Jones classics. My journey with Dr. Jones began with reading all his books. As I recall, a copy of the Indian edition of *The Christ of the Indian Road* was presented to me by Dr. Timothy C. Tennent in 2003 in Dehradun.[3] At that time, I was unaware of the legacy and significance of Jones. I have since written some academic papers about Jones, and a book about him is in process.[4]

---

1. For the most recent biography of Jones, see Robert G. Tuttle Jr., *In Our Time: The Life and Ministry of E. Stanley Jones* (Potomac, MD: The E. Stanley Jones Foundation, 2019).

2. Shivraj K. Mahendra, *A Christian History of Uttrakhand*, vol. 1, *Origins and Identities* (Delhi: ISPCK, 2014).

3. Dr. Tennent is the president and professor of world Christianity at Asbury Theological Seminary. He was my first employer in the translation ministry in 2002 and served as my mentor during my PhD studies at Asbury. He unveiled my portrait of Jones (discussed further below) in 2017.

4. The papers include "Re-Imagining Conversion and Christian Identity: Exploring E. Stanley Jones' Theology of Conversion and its Implications for Christian Identity in an Intercultural Context," paper presented at the Conference on Faith and History, Virginia Beach, Virginia, October 21, 2016; "Reformation Re-Imagined: Exploring E. Stanley Jones's Ashram Movement as a new Paradigm of Reformation in Twentieth Century Protestant Christianity," paper presented at the American Society of Church History at the 131st Annual Meeting of the American Historical Association, Denver, CO, January 5, 2017. The forthcoming book is yet to be titled.

I want to congratulate The United Methodist Publishing House for publishing the centenary edition of *The Christ of the Indian Road.* In this essay, I will explore the missional theology of E. Stanley Jones as articulated in *The Christ of the Indian Road* from the perspective of an Indian Hindu who chose, as a young adult, to follow Christ. In the process, I plan to do three things: First, engage with select themes of the book from my new "Christian" perspective. Second, explore how Dr. Jones has been a spiritual inspiration. Third, propose some implications of Jones's missiology for Christian witness in India and beyond.

Snapshots of Major Themes in *The Christ of the Indian Road*

Jones's book pursues three themes: Jones's personal experience as a missionary, his presentation of the supremacy of Christ, and his emphasis on the significance of Christian humility. These themes constitute the missiology of the book.

A Missiology of Personal Experience

Personal experience is important to Jones. The personal experience of Christ and his ministry is important to all Christians, especially to new followers of Jesus Christ. Jones decided as a young adult to follow Christ and reflected deeply on what the Lord had done in his life and is doing in the lives of others. It was from the lessons he learned in the Indian context of his ministry that he was able to define Christianity as neither Western nor Eastern, but Christ. Christ is the core of Christian missionary experience, and Christianity is about Christ.

Having defined Christianity as Christ, Jones then calls for a self-examination of the missionary. Jones describes his personal struggles and reexamines the methods of evangelism and Christian witness in India. He asserts a universal Christ and that the Christ of the Indian Road should be our message to India ("Galilean Road" 83). Jones calls for interpreting Christ in terms of Indian experiences such as those of Sadhu Sundar Singh. The Sadhu literally walked barefooted and lived like Christ, witnessing while suffering.[5] At that time, most missionaries were presenting a Western Christ; Sadhu was presenting to the world a Christ of the Indian Road. Indians have numerous philosophes, but these writers are too lofty and too abstract for the persons of the road. In *The Christ of the Indian Road,* we have a practical philosophy of the love of God for the people of the Indian Road and all roads.

A Missiology of the Supremacy of Jesus Christ

The book describes a Christocentric missiology. Jones builds his argument for the supremacy of Christ by underlining his person and Christ's moral and spiritual supremacy in the Indian context. Jones asserts, "If self-sacrifice is life's noblest quality, then run it back to its finest type and you will find yourself gazing upon a cross" (161). And upon the cross we see no one but the Lord Jesus Christ. Jones further asserts, "Jesus underlies our moral and spiritual universe deeper than the force of gravity underlies our material universe" (161). As a supreme ideal of nobility and sinlessness, it was Jesus alone who challenged the religious teachers, "Which of you can truthfully accuse me of sin?" (John 8:46 NLT).

Jones powerfully declares that "Jesus does not need to be protected. He needs to be presented" (160). This is true, and in the current context of opposition and persecution of Christians in India today, Jones prophetically provides us

5. For a brief life of the Sadhu and his experience of Christ-like life, see Shivraj K. Mahendra, "Sadhu Sundar Singh: The Apostle of the Bleeding Feet: A Study of His Experience of Persecution and Suffering for the Sake of the Gospel" in *No Turning Back: Reflections on Mission, Theology and Spirituality of Sadhu Sundar Singh*, edited by Vinod Victor and Samuel R. Saxena (Delhi: ISPCK, 2024), 157–177.

timely encouragement. We do not need to protect the gospel; we need to present it. We need not defend Christianity; we need to share it. We need not protect Christ; we need to present him. We do not need to defend the gospel; we need to live it. Christ is victorious. He is indomitable. He defeated pain, suffering, and death.

Jones approvingly cites the missionary and teacher Alfred George Hogg, who calls us to look at Jesus afresh: "Merely look at Jesus, and you behold a Man. But meet him face to face in the inwardness of comradeship and obedience, of faltering need and kingly succor, and you know yourself to be meeting the very Person, the very Self of God" (182). Summarizing the supremacy of Christ, Jones notes, "Many teachers of the world have tried to explain everything—they changed little or nothing. Jesus explained little and changed everything." And while "Many have tried to diagnose the disease of humanity—Jesus cures it" (203). Jesus is the fulfillment of all the longings of India and the world. However, Jesus must be presented in all humility.

A Missiology of Christian Humility

A good portion of the book focuses on the much-needed humility of the missionary as he or she follows Christ's example. Jesus walks on the Indian Road and uplifts India's brokenhearted, sick, and sinful to restoration. Jesus does not ride horses or elephants like the elite. He sits with the lowly. He touches the person with leprosy. This presents us with a special framework of kenotic missiology, a missiology of humility.

Jones observed that in some instances the missionaries ended up focusing on what was wrong with others. They were tempted to highlight the darkness instead of the light (John 8:12). They were mistakenly representing cultural and national superiority instead of the supremacy of Christ. Many missionaries appeared to be linked with the dominant powers, colonizers, and kings. Thus, they could be at times arrogant, rude, and even exploitative. Jesus did not come to Westernize or Easternize people. He came to love and serve them. Missionaries should be humble enough to present the humble servant, "the suffering servant." Jesus did not come to be served (Mark 10:45). We need to emulate the servant Christ. Jones's reminder is relevant today, as even after foreign missionaries are gone, some domestic missionaries seem to imitate those foreign missionaries instead of Christ.

When facing the hard questions about Christian character and Christianity in Christian-majority nations of his time, such as the United States, with its issues of discrimination and prejudice, Jones was humble enough to respond to queries and seek advice for improving his country of origin. Jones acknowledged the need for a "pervasive humility" and "deep sense of national and racial repentance" on the part of all Christians (149). We need these attitudes today.

Jones had high hopes and a twofold objective: "to strengthen and convert the church, to try to Christianize unchristian Christianity wherever found—and to win the educated non-Christians of India to an allegiance to Christ."[6] Jones carried this objective out in boldness and humility. The story of his experiences is before us as an example and an inspiration.

E. Stanley Jones: My Inspiration

Dr. Jones went to be with the Lord in 1973, five years before I was born. I have had a secondary encounter and experience with him through his books and sermons. I have also learned from others who knew him personally and were touched by him. Jones inspired me to follow Christ, and my intense study of his work has been a journey of transformation. His insights

6. E. Stanley Jones, *A Song of Ascents: A Spiritual Autobiography* (Nashville: Abingdon Press, 1968), 111.

are always fresh, inspiring, and prescient. Many of his books read as if they were written yesterday!

Jones inspires us to reach the high castes and intellectuals of India with the gospel through roundtable conferences, publications, and other media. He stood against wars and mediated peace between nations such as the United States and Japan as well as India and Pakistan. Jones also promoted mental health care for missionaries, pastors, and all those in need, which is essential in our day.

Jones also inspires us to intentionally become friends with community and political leaders. He was friends with world leaders, such as Gandhi and Nehru. He challenges us to walk like Gandhi and calls us to appreciate the Christlikeness in the non-Christians. Above all, Jones calls us to be like Sadhu Sundar Singh ji—who led a spiritually vibrant nationalistic life that positioned Christ and Christianity within the Indian context—so that through persons like the Sadhu (and E. Stanley Jones), Christ will become ever more visible on the Indian Road. According to Jones, it was the Sadhu who truly exemplified the Christian of the Indian Road with the Christ of the Indian Road. Jones inspires us in so many more ways: as a prolific writer, Christian ashram movement leader, round table conference speaker, missionary-statesman, and preacher of the cross and lover of Christ.[7]

My own pilgrimage with Christ began where the Lord Jesus found me, in the valley of death, to where He lifted me, to the shadow of the cross, where there is life beyond the grave. Jesus looks for the lost and crowns them with life everlasting. My Christian pilgrimage is the experience of the cross.[8] It was my

7. For a history of Christian ashrams, see Anne Mathews-Younes, *A History of the Christian Ashrams in North America* (Potomac, MD: The E. Stanley Jones Foundation, 2017); Anne Mathews-Younes, *A History of the Sat Tal Christian Ashram* (E. Stanley Jones Foundation, 2018).

8. I sing of this experience in my Hindi poem "Kroos Masih Ka," in *Masih Meri Manzil* (Delhi: ISPCK, 2008), 53–54.

childhood memory of the story of Christ that, when the time had come, pointed me back to Christ. When Christ appeared to me in 1996 on a fine Easter morning, it was clear that my life could not remain the same. My fear of death, which had been present from childhood due to the untimely death of my mother, was transformed into the joy of everlasting life. Jesus became my Lord, and I increasingly experienced the fullness of life. My old life was gone, and a new life had arrived. Witchcraft, drinking, and tobacco were gone. Bible, prayer, and temperance had arrived. A whole new vision had dawned on my life and mission. Jones helped to secure this new vision. From my own experience, I can underline Jones's declaration and assert that Christianity is definitely Christ, or I would have been long lost. Thank God the experience of Christ is better than the experience of Christianity, the system built around Christ. My new life is about Christ.

My gratitude to Jones inspired me to paint his portrait, which was presented to the E. Stanley Jones School of Mission and Ministry at Asbury Theological Seminary. The E. Stanley Jones Foundation includes this portrait with all of their reprinted books by E. Stanley Jones. Inspired by Jones's daily devotionals, I recently published a 365-day daily Hindi devotional, *Bible Ka Sandesh* (The message of the Bible) in 2021.[9] I owe the vision of my daily devotional to Jones, who was a prolific writer, penning more than 300 articles, 27 books, and hundreds of sermons. Jones had an anointing to share the Word, one that I long for.

Missiological Implications

A century ago, Jones had a prophetic vision for the naturalization of Christ in the Indian context. Jones knew that he did

9. Shivraj K. Mahendra, *Bible Ka Sandesh: Dainik Manan Aur Prarthana* (Delhi: ISPCK, 2021).

not bring Christ to India; Christ was already there, but Jesus was not recognized by India, for he was clothed in the garments of the Western church. Jones disentangled Christ from Western civilization and unspiritual Europeanism. Christ does walk on the Indian Road. Jesus transforms ordinary individuals into extraordinary people. Jesus is not guessing or speculating like other gurus, he is the answer. We need not protect him, only present him. This we need to do with humility and dedication. And we must constantly improve our methods of witnessing. We do not need to follow the old ways and methods of condemning the other or pointing to their faults. We only need to live our faith and witness through honest and authentic Christian living. We can benefit from a new reading of *The Christ of the Indian Road* in which we see clearly what Jones states: Christianity must be defined as Christ, not Western civilization, not even the system built around him in the West, but Christ himself, and to be a Christian is to follow him. Christ must be interpreted in terms of Christian experience rather than through mere argument.

Jones challenges us to be honest, frank, and bold about our identity and motive as Christians and representatives of Christ. Christians will do better by becoming Christ-followers and accepting one another in love and unity. We must be the agents of Christ's naturalization in India and everywhere. We must present him to Indians, both low and high, in Indian garb, and let him meet them where they are. It is therefore our privilege to present Christ alone. Let everything be about Christ. He will fix everything else.

Conclusion

Writing about the significance and supremacy of Christ is like underlining the very eternal Word. And we know that heaven and earth will pass away, but the word of Christ will not pass away (Matthew 24:35). *The Christ of the India Road* continues to make an appeal to not only India but to the world at large. The lessons from the book continue to resonate with the readers today, making it a timeless classic that remains relevant for discussion of mission and evangelism and approaches to Christian witness in India and beyond.

Shivraj K. Mahendra is Dean of Online Studies and Associate Professor of Mission Studies, New Theological College, India; General Secretary of the Church History Association of India; and Editor of History, Asian American Theological Forum. He is also an ordained elder of the Free Methodist Church. Shivraj received his PhD from Asbury Theological Seminary and is the author of "Lived Missiology: The Legacy of Ernest and Phebe Ward" (2022) and an award-winning author and translator of other books. Mahendra is from Chhattisgarh in central India. He is highly familiar with the writings of E. Stanley Jones. For the past several years, he has been the managing editor of the publishing arm of the E. Stanley Jones Foundation and has helped bring to the marketplace all newly reprinted books by E. Stanley Jones.

PREFACE

PERHAPS a few words of caution may be helpful to the reader. To those familiar with India the title of this volume may lead the reader to expect the book to be what it is not—an Indian interpretation of Christ. It is, rather, an attempt to describe how Christ is becoming naturalized upon the Indian Road.

To those who have no first-hand familiarity with conditions in India another word of caution may be given. The author has tried to be scrupulously careful not to overdraw the picture. He has let non-Christians themselves largely tell the story of the silent revolution in thought that is taking place in India. But even so, the American and English reader must be careful not always to read into the statements of the non-Christians the full content of his own thinking. In that case unwarranted implications may be drawn from them.

Christian missions have come to a crisis in India. A new and challenging situation confronts us. If we are to meet it, we must boldly follow the Christ into what are, to us, untried paths. In order to understand these modern movements, one must know the past, and must keep constantly in mind the foundations that have been laid for this new day by the patient toil and sacrificial living of generations of missionaries and Indian Christians. This book does not pretend to fill in that picture, though every moment the writer realizes the indebt-edness to those of that past who have toiled and looked for this day of broadening opportunity. In any case Christian missions are but in their beginnings in India. With adjusted attitude and spirit, they will be needed in the East for decades and generations to come.

My thanks are due to Dr. David G. Downey, who, owing to my return to India, has graciously undertaken to read the proofs and to see the book through the press.

At the request of the publishers the spoken style has been retained.

E. Stanley Jones, 1924
Mission House, Sitapur, U. P., India.

Preface to the Sixth Edition

SOME of my readers have observed the absence from this book of certain notes usual in missionary textbooks. Where, they ask, are the child-widows, the caste system with its compartmentalized and consequently paralyzed life, the six million sadhus roaming through India finding little and contributing less; is Hinduism only a philosophical system—is there not a popular side with its 330,000,000 gods and goddesses, its endless pilgrimages and rapacious priests at each stage, its worship of demons and gods of questionable character; has the purdah system been abolished; has the appalling illiteracy amounting to ninety-three per cent been wiped out? Have these dark lines, hitherto so common in the picture, faded out? Is it all sweetness and light?

No, these things are still there. But I have left them out of the picture for three reasons.

First. India is aggrieved, and I think rightly so, that Christian missionaries in order to arouse the West to missionary activity have too often emphasized the dark side of the picture. What they have said has been true, but the picture has not been a true one. This overemphasis on the one side has often created either pity or contempt in the minds of the hearers. In modern jargon a superiority complex has resulted. I do not believe a superiority complex to be the proper spring for missionary activity.

Eastern travelers in America, picking and choosing their facts, can make out a very dark picture of our civilization—the slums of our cities, the lynchings, divorce statistics, crime statistics unparalleled in other cities of the world, and so on. They have, in fact, done so. As Americans we have resented it as being an untrue picture. Then as Christians we should do unto others as we would that others should do unto us.

Second. Indians themselves are now alive to these evils and are combating them. The impact of Christian ideals upon the situation has created a conscience regarding these things and we can trust India to right them as she is, in fact, now doing. The fact is that racial lines are so drawn that India will probably deal more drastically with her evils if she does it from within than if we foreigners were always insisting upon it. As a Turkish lawyer said to us regarding the reforms in Turkey, "The things which we have done in four years no outside power or government could have made us do. We are surprised at it ourselves." The secret was that *they* did it.

Third. I have tried to lay the foundations for Christian missions deeper than upon particular evils found in a particular race. Taken at their very best, pagan men and women and systems in East or West need Christ. I have said to India very frankly: "I do not make a special drive upon you because you are the neediest people of our race, but because you are a member of our race. I am convinced that the only kind of a world worth having is a world patterned after the mind and spirit of Jesus. I am therefore making a drive upon the world as it is, on behalf of the world as it ought to be, and as you are a part of that world, I come to you. But I would not be here an hour if I did not know that ten others were doing in the land from which I come what I am trying to do here. We are all in the same deep need. Christ, I believe, can supply that need."

Another word should be added regarding another seeming lack of emphasis. I have not emphasized the mass movement among the low castes because this book has been the story growing out of my own sphere of work. My work has been more connected with that mass movement *in mind* described in these pages than with the mass movement among the low castes. Despite its obvious weaknesses and dangers, I am deeply grateful for and rejoice in this latter mass movement in which there is a turning of these voiceless[1] millions to Christ. Despite statements to the contrary, this movement is going on with unabated force. Since my return to India a friend showed a petition signed with thumb impressions by eighteen thousand of these people who desired to come into the Christian Church. But my emphasis has been upon what I knew best growing out of experience.

A further word concerning the attitudes I find on my return after an absence of nearly two years from India. I find India even more open and responsive than when I left. The mass movement *in mind* goes on in silent but unabated vigor. As the physical atmosphere becomes saturated with moisture and heavy to the point of precipitation so the spiritual atmosphere of India is becoming saturated with Christ's thoughts and ideals and is heavy to the point of precipitation into Christian forms and expression. As to when that will take place depends upon how much Christlikeness we can put into the situation. As the leading Arya Samajist in India recently said to the writer, "Everything depends upon the Christian Church." It does.

E. Stanley Jones

Mission House, Sitapur, U. P., India

1. *Voiceless* replaces E. Stanley Jones's original term *dumb* throughout the book, which had a different connotation at the time of the publication of this book in 1925.

Introduction

Clearing the Issues

WHEN the early evangelists of the Good News were sent out on their own, they returned and told Jesus "what they had done and what they had taught." This evangelist must add a third to what he has done and what he has taught—what he has learned. It will not be primarily an account of what has been done *through* him, but what has been done *to* him.

Running through it all will be the perhaps unconscious testimony of how, while speaking to India, I was led along to a simplification of my task and message and faith—and I trust of my life.

Recently at the close of an address a friend remarked, "He has probably done some good to India, but India has certainly done a great deal for him." India has. In my sharing with her what has been a gift to me I found that I had less than I thought I had—and more.

I thought my task was more complex than I now see it to be; not less difficult but less complex. When I first went to India I was trying to hold a very long line—a line that stretched clear from Genesis to Revelation, on to Western Civilization and to the Western Christian Church. I found myself bobbing up and down that line fighting behind Moses and David and Jesus and Paul and Western Civilization and the Christian Church. I was worried. There was no well-defined issue. I found the battle almost invariably being pitched at one of these three places: the Old Testament, or Western Civilization, or the Christian Church. I had the ill-defined but instinctive feeling that the heart of the matter was being left out. Then I saw that I could, and should, shorten my line, that I could take my stand at Christ and before that non-Christian world refuse to know anything save Jesus Christ and him crucified. The sheer storm and stress of things had driven me to a place that I could hold. Then I saw that there is where I should have been all the time. I saw that the gospel lies in the person of Jesus, that he himself is the Good News, that my one task was to live and to present him. My task was simplified.

But it was not only simplified—it was vitalized. I found that when I was at the place of Jesus, I was every moment upon the vital. Here at this place all the questions in heaven and earth were being settled. He was the one question that settled all others.

I still believed in the Old Testament as being the highest revelation of God given to the world before Jesus' coming; I would inwardly feed upon it as Jesus did. But the issue was further on. A Jain lawyer, a brilliant writer against Christianity, arose in one of my meetings and asked me a long list of questions regarding things in the Old Testament. I replied, "My brother, I think I can answer your questions, but I do not feel called on to do so. I defined Christianity as Christ. If you have any objections to make against him, I am ready to hear them and answer them if I can." He replied, "Who gave you this authority to make this distinction? What church council gave you this authority?" I replied that my own Master gave it to me—that I was not following a church council, but trying to follow him, and he himself had said: "Ye have heard it said of old time, . . . but I say unto you," so I was simply following his lead, for he made his own word final even in Scripture. I was bringing the battle up from that incomplete stage of Revelation to the final—to Jesus. Revelation was progressive, culminating in him. Why should I, then, pitch my battle at an imperfect stage when the perfect was here in him? My lawyer friend saw with dismay that a great many of his books written against Christianity had gone into ashes by my definition. They were beside the point. But the lawyer was not to blame for missing the point. Had we not often by our writings and by our attitudes led him to believe that we did make the issue there?

Our confusion was Peter's confusion which the Father's voice and the vision of Jesus clarified. On the Mount of Transfiguration, Moses, representing the law, and Elijah the prophets, talked with Jesus, the New Revelation. The Jewish heart of Peter wanted to keep all three and put them on the same level—he wanted to build three tabernacles for them. A voice from the cloud spoke, "This is my beloved Son; hear him"—the law and the prophets are fulfilled in him; hear him. And when they lifted up their eyes, they saw no man save Jesus only. He filled their horizon. He must fill ours.

Again, have we not often in the past led India and the non-Christian world to think that our type of civilization in the West is the issue? Before the Great War was not Western greatness often preached as a reason for the East becoming Christian? This was a false trail and led us into many embarrassments, calling for endless apologies and explanations.

There is little to be wondered at that India hesitates about our civilization—great and beautiful on certain sides and weak and ugly on others. While some of the contacts of the West with the East have been in terms of beautiful self-sacrifice and loving service, some of them have been ugly and un-Christian. But that we are not more Christian in the West is understandable when we remember in what manner much of our Christianity was propagated in Europe. Many of the evils which now afflict the West came in with it. While it is true that many of the first missionaries to the European tribes were men of rare saintliness and self-sacrifice, nevertheless Christianity was not always propagated by saintliness and self-sacrifice.

Take three illustrations that may show why three great un-Christian things lie back in our civilizations.

All Russia became Christian with Vladimir the Emperor. He desired to become a Christian, but hesitated, for, as being beneath his dignity, he would not be baptized by the local clergy. He wanted the Patriarch of Constantinople to perform the ceremony—that would give the desired dignity. But to ask him to come to do it would be receiving a bounty at the hands of another. He decided that the only thing consonant with his honor would be to conquer Constantinople and compel the Patriarch to baptize him. He would then stand as dictator and not as suppliant. That was actually carried out. Constantinople was captured and the Patriarch forced to baptize him. Thus, Russia became Christian! Is it to be wondered at that *domination* continues in the West in spite of Christianity? It came in with it.

Another. The Saxons, a warring tribe of Europe, were practically compelled by Charlemagne to become Christians. They consented on one condition. That condition would only be known at the time of their baptism. When these warriors were put under the water as a symbol that their old life was dead, they went under—all except their right arms. They held them out, lifted above their heads. These were their fighting arms. They were never Christianized! Is it to be wondered at that *war* continues in the West despite Christianity? It came in with it.

Another. The Mayflower that carried the Pilgrim Fathers to religious liberty in America went on her next trip for a load of slaves. The good ship *Jesus* was in the slave trade for our fathers. Is it to be wondered at that *race and color prejudice* still exists in the West despite Christianity? It came in with it.

The East feels that these things are still there. But standing amid the shadows of Western civilization, India has seen a

Figure who has greatly attracted her. She has hesitated regarding any allegiance to him, for India has thought that if she took one she would have to take both—Christ and Western civilization went together. She is making an amazing and remarkable discovery, namely, that Christianity and Jesus are not the same—that they may have Jesus without the system that has been built up around him in the West. That dawning revelation is of tremendous significance to them—and to us.

"Do you mean to say," said a Hindu lawyer in one of my meetings about seven years ago, "that you are not here to wipe out our civilization and replace it with your own? Do you mean that your message is Christ, without any implications that we must accept Western civilization? I have hated Christianity, but if Christianity is Christ, I do not see how we Indians can hate it." I could assure him that my message was that and only that. But this was seven years ago. That matter has now become clarified, more or less. It has become clear that we are not there to implant Western civilization.

They may take as little or as much from Western civilization as they like—and there is much that is tremendously worthwhile—but we do not make it the issue. The fact is that if we do not make it the issue, they will probably take more from it than if we did.

But the swift and often accurate intuitions of the Indian have gone further. He is making an amazing and remarkable discovery, namely, that Christianity and Jesus are not the same—that they may have Jesus without the system that has been built up around him in the West.

A prominent lecturer, who has just returned from India, says that this discovery on the part of India of the difference between Christianity and Jesus "can be called nothing less than a discovery of the first magnitude." Let it be said that the suggestion as to the difference is not new; it has been said before. But the thing that is new is that a people before their acceptance of Christianity have noted the distinction and seem inclined to act upon it. It is a most significant thing for India and the world that a great people of amazing spiritual capacities are seeing, with remarkable insight, that Christ is the center of Christianity, that utter commitment to him and catching his mind and spirit, and living his life constitute a Christian. This realization has remarkable potentialities for the future religious history of the whole race.

Looking upon it in the large, I cannot help wondering if there is not a Providence in the fact that India has not accepted Christianity *en masse* before this discovery was fixed in her mind. If she had accepted Christianity without this clarification, her Christianity would be but a pale copy of ours and would have shared its weaknesses. But with this discovery taking place before acceptance, it may mean that at this period of our racial history the most potentially spiritual race of the world may accept Christ as Christianity, may put that emphasis upon it, may restore the lost radiance of the early days when he was the center, and may give us a new burst of spiritual power.

For in all the history of Christianity whenever there has been a new emphasis upon Jesus there has been a fresh outburst of spiritual vitality and virility. As Bossuet says, "Whenever Christianity has struck out a new path in her journey it has been because the personality of Jesus has again become living, and a ray from his being has once more illuminated the world."

Out of a subject race came this gospel in the beginning, and it may be that out of another subject race may come its clarification and revivification. Some of us feel that the next great spiritual impact upon the soul of the race is due to come by way of India.

CHAPTER I

THE MESSENGER AND THE MESSAGE

I HAVE been asked to tell in this book of my evangelistic experiences in the East. I have found that all real evangelistic work begins in the evangelist. Around the world the problem of Christian work is the problem of the Christian worker. As family training cannot rise above family character, so Christian service cannot rise above the Christian servant.

I, therefore, cannot begin it in any better way than to tell of a bit of personal experience—apart from which I question whether I would have had the courage to undertake it. After over eight years continuously in India in various types of missionary work, ranging from pastor of an English church, head of a publishing house, missionary to the villages, district superintendent of large areas, I felt strangely drawn to work among the educated high castes, the intelligentsia. As a mission we were doing very little indeed among them. We had taken the line of least resistance and nearly all our work was among the low castes.

Along with my regular work I had started a Bible class and study group at an Indian club house where leading Hindus and Muslims gathered. After tennis in the evenings, we would sit together until darkness fell and study the New Testament and discuss spiritual matters. One day one of the leading government officials, a Hindu, remarked, "How long has this mission been in this city?" I told him about fifty years. He asked very pointedly: "Then why have you gone only to the low castes? Why haven't you come to us?" I replied that I supposed it was because we thought they did not want us. He replied: "It is a mistake. We want you if you will come in the right way." We want you if you will come in the right way! Almost every moment since then I have been in an eager quest for that right way. I have come to the conclusion that the right way was just to be a Christian with all the fearless implications of that term.

But who was sufficient for these things? For it meant standing down amid the currents of thought and national movements sweeping over India and interpreting Christ to the situation. I was painfully conscious that I was not intellectually prepared for it. I was the more painfully conscious that I was not Christian enough to do what the situation demanded. And most depressing of all, I was physically broken.

The eight years of strain had brought on a nervous exhaustion and brain fatigue so that there were several collapses in India before I left for furlough. On board ship while speaking in a Sunday morning service there was another collapse. I took a year's furlough in America. On my way back to India I was holding evangelistic meetings among the university students of the Philippine Islands at Manila. Several hundreds of these Roman Catholic students professed conversion. But amid the strain of the meetings my old trouble came back. There were several collapses. I went on to India with a deepening cloud upon me. Here I was beginning a new term of service in this trying climate and beginning it—broken. I went straight to the hills upon arrival and took a complete rest for several months. I came down to the plains to try it out and found that I was just as badly off as ever. I went to the hills again. When I came down the second time, I saw that I could go no further, I was at the end of my resources, my health was shattered. Here I was facing this call and task and yet utterly unprepared for it in every possible way.

I saw that unless I got help from somewhere I would have to give up my missionary career, go back to America and go to work on a farm to try to regain my health. It was one of my darkest hours. At that time, I was in a meeting at Lucknow. While in prayer, not particularly thinking about myself, a Voice seemed to say, "Are you yourself ready for this work to which I have called you?" I replied: "No, Lord, I am done for. I have reached the end of my rope." The Voice replied, "If you will turn that over to me and not worry about it, I will take care of it." I quickly answered, "Lord, I close the bargain right here." A great peace settled into my heart and pervaded me. I knew it was done! Life—abundant Life—had taken possession of me. I was so lifted up that I scarcely touched the road as I quietly walked home that night. Every inch was holy ground. For days after that I hardly knew I had a body. I went through the days, working all day and far into the night, and came down to bedtime wondering why in the world I should ever go to bed at all, for there was not the slightest trace of tiredness of any kind. I seemed possessed by Life and Peace and Rest—by Christ himself.

The question came as to whether I should tell this. I shrank from it but felt I should—and did. After that it was sink or swim before everybody. But nine of the most strenuous years of my life have gone by since then, and the old trouble has never returned, and I have never had such health. But it was more than a physical Touch. I seemed to have tapped new Life for body, mind, and spirit. Life was on a permanently higher level. And I had done nothing but take it!

I suppose that this experience can be picked to pieces psychologically and explained. It does not matter. Life is bigger than processes and overflows them. Christ to me had become *Life*.

Apart from this Touch, I question if I would have had the courage to answer the call to work among these leaders of India's thought and life. It was too big and too exacting. But here I saw my Resources. And they have not failed.

Now a word as to that right method of approach. There were two or three methods of approach then current: (1) The old method of attacking the weaknesses of other religions and then trying to establish your own on the ruins of the other. (2) The method of Doctor J. N. Farquhar, which was to show how Christianity fulfills the ancient faiths—a vast improvement on the old method. (3) The method of starting with a general subject of interest to all, and then ending up with a Christian message and appeal.

I felt instinctively that there should be a better approach than any of these three. I see now how I was feeling after it. I have before me a note written eight years ago laying down some principles I thought we should follow. (1) Be absolutely frank—there should be no camouflage in hiding one's meaning or purpose by noncommittal subjects. The audience must know exactly what it is coming to hear. (2) Announce beforehand that there is to be no attack upon anyone's religion. If there is any attack in it, it must be by the positive presentation of Christ. He himself must be the attack. That would mean that kind of attack may turn in two directions—upon us as well as upon them. He would judge both of us. This would tend to save us from feelings and attitudes of superiority, so ruinous to Christian work. (3) Allow them to ask questions at the close—face everything and dodge no difficulties. (4) Get the leading non-Christians of the city where the meetings are held to become chairmen of our meetings. (5) Christianity must be defined as Christ, not the Old Testament, not Western civilization, not even the system built around him in the West, but Christ himself and to be a Christian is to follow him. (6) Christ must be interpreted in terms of Christian experience rather than through mere argument.

That was written eight years ago. As I look back I find that we have been led forward in two most important steps since then: (1) I have dropped out the term "Christianity" from my announcements (it isn't found in the Scriptures, is it?), for it had connotations that confused, and instead I have used the name of Christ in subjects announced and in the address itself. The other way I had to keep explaining that I meant Christ by Christianity. (2) Christ must be in an Indian setting. It must be the Christ of the Indian Road. I saw that no movement would succeed in India that cuts across the growing national consciousness of India, that Christianity did seem to be cutting across that national consciousness; it was therefore not succeeding—at least among the nationally conscious classes. A leading Nationalist said to me, "I am not afraid of Christianity as such, but I am afraid of what is happening. Everyone who becomes a Christian is lost to our national cause." No wonder he suspected it. Christianity to succeed must stand, not with Cæsar, nor depend upon government backing and help, but must stand with the people. It must work with the national grain and not against it. Christ must not seem a Western Partisan of White Rule, but a Brother of Men and Women. We would welcome to our fellowship the modern equivalent of the Zealot, the nationalist, even as our Master did.

As to the manner and spirit of the presentation of that message, we should consider it of the highest importance that the penetrating statement of Rabindranath Tagore should be kept in mind that "when missionaries bring their truth to a strange land, unless they bring it in the form of homage it is not accepted and should not be. The manner of offering it to you must not be at all discordant with your own national thought and your self-respect." I felt that we who come from a foreign land should have the inward feeling, if not the outward signs, of being adopted sons and daughters of India, and we should offer our message as a homage to our adopted land; respect should characterize our every attitude; India should be home, her future our future, and we her servants for Jesus' sake.

We have come, then, this far in our thinking: that the Christ of the Indian Road, with all the fullness of meaning that we can put into those words, should be our message to India.

That this centering of everything in Jesus is the right lead is remarkably corroborated by Doctor Charles W. Gilkey, the Barrows lecturer, who has just returned from a great hearing in India. After consultation with a great many, of whom I was honored to be one, he chose as the subject for the lectures, "The Personality of Jesus." To choose such a subject was in itself an adventure. A leading Christian college president in India said to Doctor Gilkey: "If you had chosen that subject as recently as five years ago, or even three, you would have had no hearing. I am as much amazed as you are at this burst of interest and these crowds." The leading Hindu social thinker of India, commenting in his paper, remarked, "The Barrows lecturer could not have chosen a subject of more vital interest in India today than the subject, 'The Personality of Jesus.'" It was good to find my own experience corroborated in the experience of another.

Hitherto it has been exceedingly difficult to get non-Christians to come to a Christian address of any kind. But in —— the most prominent Hindu, a Muslim judge, and a Christian missionary signed the notices that went out calling the meetings. To me at that time it was a new experience to have them do it. An experienced missionary said to me after one of the meetings, "If you had told me a week ago that the leading men of this city would sit night after night listening to the straightest gospel one could present and ask for more, I would not have believed it, and yet they are doing it." I have found that they will listen when that gospel is Christ and are drawn when he is lifted up.

It may be that we will yet discover that good Christianity is good tactics, that the straightforward, open proclamation of Jesus is the best method. Paul believed this, for he says, "I disown those practices which very shame conceals from view; I do not go at it craftily, I do not falsify the word of God; I state the truth openly and so commend myself to every man's conscience in the sight of God. . . . It is Christ Jesus as Lord, not myself, that I proclaim" (2 Corinthians 4:2-5, MNT). Paul let Jesus commend himself to every person's conscience, for he knew that Jesus appeals to the soul as light appeals to the eye, as truth fits the conscience, as beauty speaks to the aesthetic nature. For Christ and the soul are made for one another, and when they are brought together, deep speaks to deep and wounds answer wounds.

That this approach is probably sound is seen by the statement of the non-Christian chairman who rebuked a Christian speaker because he had tried to come at it gradually: "We can speak of God ourselves, we expect to hear from you about Christ."

We often quote Paul's speech at Athens as a model of missionary approach and yet it was one of Paul's biggest failures. He did not succeed in founding a church there. Mackintosh analyzes his failure thus: "The Christian propaganda failed or prospered in proportion as the fresh data for religion present in Jesus were studiously concealed or openly proclaimed. Take Paul's address at Athens: [it] says some fine things, God's spirituality, a God afar off—one in whom we live and move, creation instead of chaos. Providence instead of chance, men of one blood instead of proud distinction between Greek and Barbarian. But at no point is publicity given to the distinctive Christian message. In this studied omission of the cross is the secret of his comparative failure at Athens and his subsequent change at Corinth. He writes penitently, 'I determined to know nothing among you save Jesus Christ and him crucified.' The gospel had lost its savor when it was merged in Jewish commonplace."[1]

But the Hindu insists, and rightly so, that it must not be "an incrusted Christ," to use the words of the student representative before the World's Student Conference at Peking [now Beijing]. It must not be a Christ bound with the grave clothes of long-buried doctrinal controversy, but a Christ as fresh and living and as untrammeled as the one that greeted Mary at the empty tomb on that first Easter morning.

A Hindu puts the matter thus: "We have been unwilling to receive Christ into our hearts, but we alone are not responsible for this. . . . Christian missionaries have held out to us a Christ completely covered by their Christianity. Up to now their special efforts have been to defeat our religious doctrines, and therefore we have been prepared to fight in order to self-defense. Men cannot judge when they are in a state of war. In the excitement of that intoxication, while intending to strike the Christians, we have struck Jesus Christ."[2]

But we too must acknowledge our part in the mistake and see to it that in the future India has a chance to respond to an untrammeled Christ.

A friend of mine was talking to a Brahman gentleman when the Brahman turned to him and said, "I don't like the Christ of your creeds and the Christ of your churches." My friend quietly replied, "Then how would you like the Christ of the Indian Road?" The Brahman thought a moment, mentally picturing the Christ of the Indian Road—he saw him dressed in Sadhus' garments, seated by the wayside with the crowds about him, healing blind men who felt their way to him, putting his hands upon the heads of poor, unclean lepers who fell at his feet,

1. H. R. Mackintosh, *The Originality of the Christian Message* (New York: Scribner, 1920), 23–24.

2. W. E. S. Holland, *The Goal of India* (London: Church Missionary Society, 1918), 206.

announcing the good tidings of the Kingdom to stricken folks, staggering up a lone hill with a broken heart and dying upon a wayside cross for humanity, but rising triumphantly and walking on that road again. He suddenly turned to the friend and earnestly said, "I could love and follow the Christ of the Indian Road."

How differs this Christ of the Indian Road from the Christ of the Galilean Road? Not at all.

Christ is becoming a familiar Figure upon the Indian Road. He is becoming naturalized there. Upon the road of India's thinking you meet with him again and again, on the highways of India's affection you feel his gracious Presence, on the ways of her decisions and actions he is becoming regal and authoritative. And the voice of India is beginning to say with Whittier:

> "The healing of the seamless dress
> Is by our beds of pain;
> We touch him in life's throng and press,
> And we are whole again."[3]

---

3. J. G. Whittier (lyrics 1866), "Immortal Love, Forever Full," in *The Book of Hymns: Official Hymnal of the United Methodist Church* (Nashville: United Methodist Publishing House, 1966; 15th printing, 1979), no. 157–58.

CHAPTER II

THE MOTIVE AND END OF CHRISTIAN MISSIONS

THERE is a good deal of misunderstanding as to why we are undertaking Christian missions and as to what we are really trying to do. A very severe criticism is beating upon this whole question of missions from many angles and sources. Personally, I welcome it. If what we are doing is real, it will shine even more. If it isn't real, the sooner we find it out the better.

We have been called international meddlers, creed mongers to the East, feverish ecclesiastics compassing land and sea to gain another proselyte. From the other side comes the criticism that we satisfy a racial superiority complex when we go on helpful service to other nations; that we are the kindly side of imperialism—we go ahead and touch the situation in terms of schools and hospitals and human helpfulness, then imperialism comes along and gathers up the situation in the name of empire; or that capitalism takes over and exploits the situation as intrepid missionaries open it up. Again it is said that it is a bit of spiritual impertinence to come to a nation that can produce a Gandhi or a Tagore. Finally, we are told that the whole missionary movement is a mistake, since, as non-Christian investigators tell us, the last command of Jesus to go into the world and preach the gospel is an interpolation, hence the whole is founded upon a mistaken idea.

These are serious criticisms and must be met fairly and squarely. If this whole question of missions is to hold the affections of the church in the future, we must be sure that we are about a business that commends itself to the mind as well, for what does not hold the mind will soon not hold the heart. Besides, let it be noted that if Christianity isn't worth exporting it isn't worth keeping. If we cannot share it, we cannot keep it.

Some of the motives that were valid in the past are not holding good today. In the days when I volunteered to be a missionary the prevailing thought was that here is a cataract of human souls pouring over into perdition and that we were to rescue as many as possible. Rightly or wrongly, this idea is no longer prevailing as a motive for foreign missions. Then at the close of the Great War there was the feeling that democracy was the panacea for the world's ills, and that America, being the embodiment of the democratic ideal, should loose democracy, permeated with Christianity, upon the world. A good deal of the thought underlying the Methodist Centenary and the Interchurch World Movement was pervaded with this idea. We now see that democracy, fine as it is, is no panacea for the world's diseases, that paralyzing evils can flourish in a democracy as flagrantly as in an autocracy. A thoughtful Hindu, after reading Lord James Bryce's *Modern Democracies*, put it down and remarked to a friend, "After all, democracy is only an ideal, and that ideal will never be realized until the kingdom of God comes on earth as it is in heaven." We must go deeper than democracy.

Then there was a time when we thought we were there in the East to Westernize it in general. I remember very vividly an address given twenty years ago by a prominent Christian editor, on the lines,

> "Out of the darkness of night
> The world rolls into light.
> It is daybreak everywhere."[1]

The whole address was a recounting of electric cars in Bombay [now Mumbai], and American plows in Africa and dress suits in Japan as a sign that it is daybreak everywhere! I am frank to say that I would not turn over my hand to Westernize the East, but I trust I would give my life to Christianize it. It cannot be too clearly said that they are not synonymous. We have seen as by a lurid flash during this last war that much of our civilization is still held under the sway of pagan ideals. Who was it that prayed, "Oh, to see the world with the lid off"? Well, we have seen it with the lid off, and the grim form of our pagan past leered out of the depths at us. That pagan past was controlling much of the submerged life of our outwardly brilliant civilization. To see many of our modern cities with the lid off would cure us of an easy optimism. No, paganism is not a thing to which we can point on the map and say, "It is here," "It is there." It is not a geographical something, but a matter of the spirit, and there may be vast areas of thought and purpose and spirit that are still pagan on both sides of the world. Paganism may be either in East or West.

As yet there is no such thing as a Christian nation. There are Christianized individuals and groups, but the collective life of no people has been founded upon the outlook of Jesus. We are only partially Christianized. That does not mean that we are not appreciative of and thankful for the Christianization that has taken place, nor are we blind to the fact that our civilization is probably the best that has been produced so far in human history, but we are not measuring ourselves by ourselves, but in the white light of the person of Jesus.

1. Henry Wadsworth Longfellow, "The Bells of San Blas" (1882).

We want the East to keep its own soul—only thus can it be creative. We are not there to plaster Western civilization upon the East, to make it a pale copy of ourselves. We must go deeper—infinitely deeper—than that.

Again, we are not there to give its people a blocked-off, rigid, ecclesiastical, and theological system, saying to them, "Take that in its entirety or nothing." Jesus is the gospel—he himself is the good news. Men went out in those early days and preached Jesus and the resurrection—a risen Jesus. But just as a stream takes on the coloring of the soil over which it flows, so Christianity in its flowing through the soils of the different racial and national outlooks took on coloring from them. We have added a good deal to the central message—Jesus. Some of it is worth surviving, for it has come out of reality. Some of it will not stand the shock of transplantation. It is a shock to any organism to be transplanted. I have seen a good many star preachers visit the East and have their messages translated. The result has often been disastrous. After the rhetoric and fine periods had been eliminated as untranslatable there was not enough basis of ideas to go over to be reclothed in another language. Some of our ecclesiastical systems built upon a controversy lose meaning when they pass over into a totally different atmosphere. But Jesus is universal. He can stand the shock of transplantation. He appeals to the universal heart.

We will put our civilization and our ecclesiastical systems at the disposal of India to take as much as may suit their purposes. But we do not insist upon these. We will give them Christ and urge them to interpret him through their own genius and life. Then the interpretation will be first-hand and vital.

If this viewpoint hurts our denominational pride, it may help our Christianity.

If we are not in India to do these things, just for what purpose are we there? We believe there are three great elemental needs of East and West: an adequate goal for character; a free, full life; God. We believe that Jesus in a supreme way gives these three things.

Each system must be judged by its output, its fruit. "The outcome is the criterion." What are we trying to produce? The ends of the different systems of thought and faith may be summed up as follows: Greece said, "Be moderate—know thyself"; Rome said, "Be strong—order thyself"; Confucianism says, "Be superior—correct thyself"; Shintoism says, "Be loyal—suppress thyself"; Buddhism says, "Be disillusioned—annihilate thyself"; Hinduism says, "Be separated—merge thyself"; Islam says, "Be submissive—assert thyself"; Judaism says, "Be holy—conform thyself"; Modern Materialism says, "Be industrious—enjoy thyself"; Modern Dilettantism says, "Be broad—cultivate thyself"; Christianity says, "Be Christlike—give thyself."

If the end and motive of Christianity, and therefore of Christian missions, is to produce Christlike character, I have no apology for being a Christian missionary, for I know nothing higher for God or man than to be Christlike.

I know nothing higher for God. If God in character is like Jesus, he is a good God and trustable. The present-day doubt is not concerning Christ but concerning God. Humanity wonders if there can be a good God back of things when they see earthquakes wipe out the innocent and the guilty alike and innocent little children suffer from nameless diseases, they did not bring on themselves. But the distracted and doubting mind turns toward Jesus with relief and says, "If God is like that, he is all right." As Christians we affirm that he is—that he is Christlike in character, and we say it without qualification and without the slightest stammering of the tongue. We believe that "God is Jesus everywhere" and Jesus is God here—the human life of God.

If God thinks in terms of little children as Jesus did, cares for the leper, the outcaste, and the blind, and if his heart is like that gentle heart that broke upon the cross, then he can have my heart without reservation and without question.

If the finest spirits of humanity should sit down and think out the kind of a God they would like to see in the universe, his moral and spiritual likeness would gradually form like unto the Son of Man. The greatest news that has ever been shared with humanity is the news that God is like Christ. And the greatest news that we can share to that non-Christian world is just that—that the God whom you have dimly realized, but about whose character you are uncertain, is like Christ. I have watched the look of incredulity come into the faces of men and women in India as that announcement is made. But incredulity gives way to the thought that God *ought* to be like that, and that in turn to the thought that he *is*. "I have thrown over everything in my belief as to the future life," said one of the most brilliant Hindus, "except the continuity of human existence and the consistency of the character of God." The consistency of the character of God had been fixed for him by Jesus, concerning whom he said to me, "Jesus is the highest expression of God we have ever seen." That consistency of the character of God is fleeting and intangible until Jesus fixes it forever in the soul.

Further, I know nothing higher for man than to be Christlike. The highest adjective descriptive of character in any language is the adjective "Christlike." No higher compliment can be paid to human nature than to be called Christlike. When India, a non-Christian nation, wanted to pay her highest compliment to her highest son, she searched for the highest term she knew and called Gandhi a Christlike man.

We thoughtfully throw down this ideal before the philosophers of the world, the statesmen, the moralists, the reformers, the religious thinkers, and we say to them: "Brother men, this is what we are trying to produce. We think it is worthwhile to produce Christlike character. Do you know anything finer and better? Do you know of any nobler goal? Is there any pattern which you have conceived that surpasses this in being just what life ought to be? If so, show us, and before God, we will leave this and seek the other." I believe that the lips of the world are mute and silent before the question of finding anything better. In the realm of character Jesus has the field. In the struggle and clash of ideals for human life his is the fittest to survive. Men and women need a goal for character and Jesus is that goal.

But men and women need more than a goal, they need a free, full life, for life is crippled and dwarfed. A Jewish lady in India said to the writer: "You talk to these people of religion. What they need is bread. Look how starved and pinched they are. Why don't you give them bread?" India does need bread and needs it desperately. No one can stand amid the appalling poverty of India with the average per capita income less than five cents a day, and where forty million people have never known a full stomach and will never know it from birth to death, and not feel the desperate need of helping India to get bread—more of it and quickly. Our industrial schools, our experimental farms, our cooperative banks, and numerous other endeavors at economic uplift prove that we are keenly alive to the need of helping India get bread.

But a great, unbiased economist concluded that "almost every economic evil in India is rooted in religious and social custom." Every time you try to lift India economically you run into a custom that balks you. Therefore, while I thank God for every endeavor to help India to get more bread, I believe that the best way to give India bread is to give her Christ. For Christ makes life *free*.

Moreover, I want to see India politically free. This does not mean that India must necessarily be without the British Empire. I personally hope that she will remain within it. But without self-determination India will not make her real contribution to the world. Sir John Robert Seeley was right when he said that "moral deterioration is bound to set in in any subject race." While I believe that England has given India as good government as one nation is capable of giving to another, nevertheless, I am convinced with the nationalist that "good government is no substitute for self-government." I want to see India stand upon her own feet. But the real shackles that bind India are within. Loose her there and freedom from without is that moment assured.

After Mahatma Gandhi's release from prison, I asked him what, in his opinion, was the reason for the collapse of his movement while he was in jail. He threw the question back on me and asked me what I thought was the cause. I replied that I thought that since life finally came to the level of the habitual thinking, the cause lay back in the thinking of India. In the mind of the Muslim there is gripping him in the inmost places the thought of Kismet—everything is predestined by the sovereign will of Allah. When he gets under difficulties, the tendency is to tap his forehead and say: "What can I do? My Kismet is bad." It is more or less fatalistic. On the other hand, the Hindu has lying back in his mind the thought of Karma—that we are in the grip of the results of the deeds of the previous birth. When the Hindu runs against difficult situations he usually says: "What can I do? my Karma is bad." It too is more or less fatalistic and consequently paralyzing. I suggested to the Mahatma that under the spell of his personality India forgot both Kismet and Karma and was creative, the national life was purified, and impossible things accomplished. But when he was taken away the older and deeper ideas of Kismet and Karma reasserted themselves, and under the difficulties that confronted her India sat down. The movement collapsed. I suggested that, as he well knew and practiced in a wonderful way, there was a third ideal of life, namely the cross. Now the cross never knows defeat, for it itself is Defeat, and you cannot defeat Defeat. You cannot break Brokenness. It starts with defeat and accepts that as a way of life. But in that very attitude it finds its victory. It never knows when it is defeated, for it turns every impediment into an instrument, and every difficulty into a door, every cross into a means of redemption. So, I concluded, any people that would put the cross at the center of its thought and life would never know when it is defeated. It would have a quenchless hope that Easter morning lies just behind every Calvary. It was therefore my considered belief that India will never permanently rise until both Kismet and Karma are replaced in the mind of India by the cross.

As Doctor Tagore puts it, "Things come up to a certain place in India and then stop." The reason for this I feel to be in the above. Almost every economic, social, and national evil roots back in cramping custom. I believe, therefore, that the best way to make India free economically, socially, and politically is to give her Christ.

India has always had the genius for addition, she has lacked elimination. She has absorbed everything that has come along, but she has eliminated little, hence her life is burdened and crushed. Life depends almost as much upon elimination as upon absorption. India needs a dynamic power to help her cleanse, to let go.

> The women of a lowly caste in Gujarat
> Upon each succeeding birthday add to ankles
> And to arms a ring of heavy brass until when age
> Creeps on, weighted down through life with this
> Accumulation of the years, they totter to their tasks,
> And then the burning ghat and the dreadful realms
>   of Yama.
> Custom decrees it shall be so.
>
> Thus I saw our aged India weighted down with
> Accumulated custom and sapping superstition,
> With scarce strength left to lift herself
> To stand upright among the nations.

She raised her eyes, weary, but spiritual still,
Full upon me and seemed to say,
"Adopted son of mine, if your love be true
Loose from me these weights and set me free,
For I would serve, but mind, my son, be gentle,
For by long association they seem a part of me."

O, master of my heart, give to me the touch of
Gentle power that I may help to loose our Bharat,
Mindful every moment how thy nail-pierced Hand
Didst gently loose my shackled soul
From many a chain of lust and clinging selfishness
And bade my happy soul be free.

I believe that the dynamic that India needs is Christ. Whom the Son makes free is free indeed. India needs a free, full life. And Christ is *Life*.

But more, the deepest need of the human heart East or West is God. The Indian people are the most God-stirred people on earth. But the impression I gather is that it is a stirring rather than a possession.

The whole situation was summed up to me in this scene: I was sitting in the cool of a wonderful Indian evening with an old philosopher. He was the finest type of India's thinkers, deeply read in his own philosophy and acquainted with the philosophy of the West. The spell of the quietness and calm of the evening was upon us as we discussed the questions of God, life, and destiny. In the midst of the conversation, he slowly stroked his beard and said, "I am that Ultimate Reality, but I do not know it yet." As I sat there meditating upon his words I seemed to see before me India sitting and through the voice of the old man affirming, as she has affirmed through the centuries: "I am that Ultimate Reality," and adding, "but I do not know it yet."

A few days later I saw him again. He was distressed and burdened. "My country is not free. She is divided and paralyzed. I can't seem to see any hope." Such was the burden of his plaint that day. His heart would respond to no other note.

The next day I came again, and he was radiant. "Oh," he said, "my heart has been so happy today. All day long the prayer that ——— gave us has been ringing through my mind, 'Thou art our Father, teach us how to know thee as Father.' Oh, that is it. I have peace today. That is what my country needs." But before he was through, he added with a little touch of sadness, I thought: "If this will only stay. But it doesn't seem to stay."

Do you get the picture: India affirms, "I am that Ultimate Reality," but adds, "I do not know it yet," and then finding no foothold in or power from that Impersonal Essence termed Ultimate Reality, sinks into despair concerning the real world about her: "My country—is there any hope?" Then there is the lighted-up moment when she sees a glimpse of the Father and exclaims: "Oh, that is it. I have peace today. This is what my country needs," and then plaintively ends with, "It doesn't seem to stay."

Just what is lacking there? Certainly not fine philosophic earnestness and spiritual receptivity. But when it comes down to the place of joyously getting hold, it eludes. Was there any need for Christ there? Could he do anything in that situation? As India asks with Philip, "Show us the Father and it sufficeth us," would he not stand and quietly say, "He that hath seen me hath seen the Father" (John 14:8-9)? Would he not fix the fleeting vision of the Father and make it a permanent experience of life? And out of that possession of the Father would there not grow the dynamic that would help one not to despair of conditions around one? Would not that lighted-up moment become a part of life itself? The innermost depths of my being cry out that this is so!

It is a fact of experience that when you deepen the Christ-consciousness you deepen the God-consciousness. Jesus does not push out or rival God; the more I know of him, the more I know of the Father. I do not argue that I simply testify.

Now, if any people on earth should have found God apart from Jesus Christ, the Indian people have earned that right. They have searched for God as no other nation on earth has ever searched for God. If sheer persistence of search could have found God in joyous clearness, then the Indian people have earned that right.

But it is precisely this lack of the joyous sense of finding that strikes me as I go about India. "You are the boldest man I have ever seen," said a Hindu after an address. "You said you had found God. I have never heard a man say that before." There was no credit to me—not the slightest. I had looked into the face of Jesus and lo, I saw the Father! But India has not had that face to look into, and therefore the vision of the Father is fleeting.

If this sounds dogmatic, then let India herself speak. My friend Holland gives this illuminating incident: He had had a discussion with an able Hindu judge and the judge had got the better of the argument, so he said in a kindly way: "Well, after all, there is not much difference between us. You Christians are converted when you find God in Christ. We Hindus are converted when we find God in ourselves." "With this difference," replied Holland, "that in those countries where Christ is known, conversions happen. I could take you to visit hundreds of my Christian friends in this city, Indian and English, and as you talked to them you would gather just this impression of light and discovery and inspiration of which we have been speaking, whereas I do not know of a single Hindu student that gives me the impression he has found." The judge's face fell, his tone dropped, and he said to Holland, quietly: "You are perfectly right. I know more Hindus than you, Aryas,

Brahmos, Theosophists and Orthodox; I do not know one who has found."[2]

With the exception of one man who said he was a *jiwan-mukta*, that is, one who has found living salvation, a man whom the audience smiled upon and did not take seriously, I have found India God-stirred, but still seeking. There is not yet that sense of finding.

But Jesus actually does give men and women just *that*. More, he gives a goal for character and a free, full life. Is there anyone else who can give men and women those three things? Is there anyone else actually doing it?

I asked an earnest Hindu one day what he thought of Christ. He thoughtfully answered: "There is no one else who is seriously bidding for the heart of the world except Jesus Christ. There is no one else on the field."

Sweep the horizon—is there anyone else?

Yes, Mrs. Annie Besant announces a coming World Teacher. She puts forth Krishnamurti, a Brahman youth who is to be the incarnation of Christ. (Even here she naïvely acknowledges the supremacy of Jesus, for it is to be an incarnation of *Christ*.) He has given forth his first installment of world teaching and has received divine honors in India and in the West. I had a long interview with him, found him of average intelligence, of rather lovable disposition, of mediocre spiritual intuitions, and heard him swear in good, round English! I came away feeling that if he is all we, as a race, have to look to to get out of the muddle we are in, then God pity us.

There is literally no one else on the field and nothing else on the horizon. It is Christ or—nothing. Matthew Arnold says: "Try all the ways to peace and welfare you can think of, and

2. William Edward Sladen Holland, *The Goal of India* (London: Council for Missionary Education, 1918), 209–10.

you will find that there is no way that brings you to it except the way of Jesus. But this way does bring you to it."

What, then, have we in Christianity that is not found in any of the other systems? I was asked by an ardent Arya Samajist that very question. "What have you in your religion that we haven't in ours?" He expected me to argue with him the question concerning what moral ideas and philosophic principles we had that they did not have. I answered, "Shall I tell you in a word? *You have no Christ*." Just there is the great lack of the non-Christian faiths. Fine things in their culture and thought—we admit it and thank God in real sincerity for them—but the real lack, the lack for which nothing else can atone, is just—Christ. They have no Christ. And lacking him, life lacks its supreme necessity.

Sadhu Sunder Singh, the great Christian mystic, clarifies this in his conversation with a European professor of comparative religions in a Hindu college. The professor was an agnostic as far as Christianity was concerned and interviewed the Sadhu with the evident intention of showing him his mistake in renouncing another faith for Christ. He asked, "What have you found in Christianity that you did not have in your old religion?"

The Sadhu answered, "I have Christ."

"Yes, I know," the professor replied, a little impatiently, for he was hoping for a philosophical argument, "but what particular principle or doctrine have you found that you did not have before?"

The Sadhu replied, "The particular thing I have found is Christ."

Try as the professor might, he could not budge him from that position. He went away discomfited—and thoughtful. The Sadhu was right. The non-Christian faiths have fine things in them, but they lack—Christ.

But someone objects: "Aren't they getting along pretty well without Christ?" My answer is that I know of no one, East or West, who is getting along pretty well without Christ. Christ being Life is a necessity to life.

A Brahman came to me confidentially one day and said, "Your addresses have been very much enjoyed, but there is one thing I would suggest. If you will preach Christ as *a* way, all right, but say that there may be other ways as well. If you do this, India will be at your feet." I replied, thanking my brother for his concern, but said: "I am not looking for popularity, and it is not a question what I should say. It is a question of what are the facts. They have the final word." I should be glad, more than glad, if I could say that there are others who are saving men, but I know of only One to whom I dare actually apply the term "Savior." But I do dare apply it to Christ unreservedly and without qualification. A Hindu said to me one day, "You are such a broad-minded Christian." I replied: "My brother, I am the narrowest man you have come across. I am broad on almost anything else, but on the one supreme necessity for human nature I am absolutely narrowed by the facts to one—Jesus." It is precisely because we believe in the absoluteness of Jesus that we can afford to take the more generous view of the non-Christian systems and situations. But the facts have driven us to Jesus as the supreme necessity for all life everywhere.

We disclaim, then, that this is international meddling. There is no more meddling in this than when Copernicus discovered a center around which our planet revolved and shared his discovery. It caused upset and heart-burnings to many who thought the geocentric view was sacrosanct. We now see that the disorderliness caused by this announcement was nothing compared to the vast and incurable disorderliness which was everywhere when men were thinking away from the center. We announce that we believe that we have discovered the center of this moral and spiritual universe—the person of Jesus. That causes confusion and upset. But when humanity once finds that center, they find that an orderly spiritual universe comes out of chaos. But we do not impose it upon humanity, we share it with them.

We also repudiate the idea of gaining mere members; we want character, and if there is any feverishness in our effort, it is that we are feverishly trying to set our own house in order. We need it as much as anyone else.

As for the satisfying a racial superiority complex and being the forerunners of imperialism and capitalism, let us say that Jesus is the one Figure that stands blocking every road of political and economic exploitation in the East. He is troubling exploiters everywhere. He has got hold of them. They cannot grab and exploit with quite so easy a conscience as they once did. Moreover, amid the racial clashes and bitterness there stands one who is the Son of man. Racialism withers under his real touch. He is the Friend of Men and Women.

When we are told that India produces her great men, Gandhi and Tagore, and that it is therefore impertinent to go to the East, we reply thanking God for the greatness of these sons of India; we are proud of them and grateful for them, and grateful also for the part that Jesus is having in molding them into greatness.

As for the "Great Commission" being an interpolation, we reply that this has not yet been proved; but even if it were, we would still be committed to this whole enterprise of sharing him with the world, for it is not based on a command, but upon the very nature of the gospel itself, upon him. Last command or no last command, we must share Jesus, for the necessities of human life command us to give a Savior such as Jesus. Out of the deep necessities comes the imperious voice, "Go into all the world and preach the gospel." If we hold our peace, the stones—the hard, bare facts of life—will cry out.

Further. He and the facts not only command us to go, but he, standing in the East, beckons us to come. Jesus is there—deeply there, before us. We not only take him; we go to him. Of this vivid and tragic truth, he gives us a vision in that glimpse of the last day: "I was an hungered, and ye gave me meat; I was thirsty, and ye gave me drink; I was a stranger, and ye took me in: naked, and ye clothed me: I was sick, and ye visited me: I was in prison, and ye came unto me" (Matt. 25:35-36). The righteous cry, "Lord, when saw we thee an hungered, and fed thee? or thirsty, and gave thee drink?" (25:38). The amazing words fall from his lips: "Inasmuch as ye have done it unto one of the least of these . . . ye have done it unto me" (25:45). Whom do we feed when we feed the hungry of India? That pinched man before me? Yes, and more—our own Christ is hungry in that man. And when I put the chalice to the parched lips of India—to whose lips do I put it? That man athirst before me? Yea, more, for my own Christ is again athirst in him. I do not have to take Christ to India—he is there in the perpetual incarnation of human need. When we do it to them, we do it to him. "This whole question is vascular: cut it anywhere and it will bleed."

If Christ is in this, I do not see how we can be out of it.

To sum up: We are sharing Jesus because Christlike character is the highest that we know, because he gives human beings a free, full life, and, most important of all, he gives them God. And we do not know of anyone else who does do these things except Christ. But he does.

And to the heart that has learned to love him it is irresistible to think of him hungry, thirsty, sick, in prison, naked and a stranger in the throbbing needs of our brothers and sisters.

We take them Christ—we go to him. He is the motive and the end.

CHAPTER III

The Growing Moral and Spiritual Supremacy of Jesus

MANY who have looked for the Kingdom to come only by observation so that they could say "Lo, here," and "Lo, there," have been disappointed to find it come so slowly, but the more discerning have suddenly awakened to find that the Kingdom was in the midst of them and all around them. Christianity is breaking out beyond the borders of the Christian Church and is being seen in most unexpected places. If those who have not the spirit of Jesus are none of his, no matter what outward symbols they possess, then conversely those who have the spirit of Jesus are his, no matter what outward symbols they may lack. In a spiritual movement like that of Jesus it is difficult and impossible to mark its frontiers. Statistics and classifications lose their meaning and are impotent to tell who are in and who are not. Jesus told us it would be so.

He said that the Kingdom would come in two great ways: It would be like a grain of mustard seed, a tiny thing that grows into a great tree: this speaks of the outward growth of Christianity—humanity coming into the organized expression of the Kingdom, namely, the Christian Church. Again, it would be like leaven which would silently permeate the whole: this tells of the silent permeation of the minds and hearts of men and women by Christian truth and thought until, from within, but scarcely knowing what is happening, the spirit and outlook of men and women would be silently leavened by the spirit of Jesus—they would be Christianized from within.

We see these two things taking place with the impact of Christ upon the soul of the East.

We need not stop long at the first, though the growth by that method has been very considerable. In the last ten years the population in India has increased by 1.2 per cent, but the growth of the Christian Church has been 22.6 per cent. We have added about 100,000 souls to the Christian Church every year for the last ten years—about a million in ten years. These have been largely from the outcaste sections of society. There are 60,000,000 who are called Dalit.[1] These Dalits, who have lived on the edges of life, degraded and despised, are being stirred with new virile thinking. Hitherto they have been oppressed and have opened not their mouths. But not so now. They are catching from the high-caste leaders of the Nationalist Movement (beautiful irony!) the possibilities of passive resistance and are turning it against the Brahmans themselves. Last March a year ago began a struggle in South India that has had nation-wide consequences. Some of these Dalits appeared on a forbidden road in Travancore [today primarily part of Kerala], the most caste-ridden section of India. They were promptly sent off to jail. The next day there was another group there ready to be sent off. That struggle has been going on for over a year. They go to jail, serve their sentence, and then quietly come back and sit upon the forbidden road—and India has an amazing power to sit! The sight of these silent, patient, passive resisters has shaken the caste system to its foundation, and has so stirred the high castes that some of the more sympathetic spirits among them formed

1. *Dalit* replaces E. Stanley Jones's original term *untouchables*, which was popularly used at the time of the publication of this book in 1925.

a procession a thousand strong, walked on foot one hundred fifty miles, holding meetings to arouse sympathy as they went, and presented to her Highness the ruler of Travancore a petition asking that all the roads be thrown open to the Dalits. The latest word says that these low castes had won out and the roads had been thrown open. Patient suffering had won!

These outcastes are on the move. They are debating far into the night in their caste councils as to where they will find their spiritual destiny and destination. They are talking over the relative merits of Hinduism, Islam, Buddhism (for Buddhism is being brought back into India from which it had been driven, in order, I presume, to provide a figure that is Indian to set over against the personality of Jesus) and Christianity. In the next ten or twenty years the spiritual destiny of a vast section of humankind will probably be settled. This quest of the outcaste is one of the most remarkable spiritual phenomena at the present time, for sixty million are on the move!

But there is a more remarkable movement at the other end of society among the higher castes. The movement among the low castes is called the Mass Movement; this other movement I would call a mass movement in mind toward Christ as a Person. Do not misunderstand me, they are not knocking at the doors for baptism, nor are they enamored of our ecclesiastical systems or our civilization, but there is an amazing turning in thought toward Christ. Now, "whatever gets your attention finally gets you," and I do not think I overstate or exaggerate when I say that Jesus is getting the attention of the finest minds and spirits in India—and he is getting them.

If one asks for the evidence of this, I would find it difficult to put my finger upon it, for some of it is so subtle that one has to stand down amid these swirling currents of India's life and feel a subtle change from bitterness and hate to understanding sympathy and inward love and allegiance. I can only throw open little windows through things that may seem insignificant in themselves, but which may let one see into a larger situation.

A few years ago, I was talking to a devoted English missionary who was confused and discouraged about the national situation. She wondered of what use it was to try any more to do Christian work in India since Britain had lost moral hold upon India. There was such bitterness everywhere, and she could feel it. We talked about the inner meaning of what she was experiencing and I told her of what I had seen. I shall never forget the look on her face as she said: "I see the light. Christ is bigger than my empire, and his kingdom may come either through it or in spite of it. I see light bursting through these clouds that have hung over me." A little window had let her see a great light.

Nine years ago, in the National Congress at Poona [now Pune] a Hindu gentleman in addressing the Congress used the name of Christ. There was such an uproar and confusion that he had to sit down unable to finish his speech. That name of Christ stood for all that India hated, for he was identified with empire and the foreign rulers. He had not yet become naturalized upon the Indian Road. But in the meantime, a disassociation of Jesus from the West had been made, so that nine years later when that same National Congress met, the Hindu president in giving his presidential address quoted great passages from the New Testament, took out bodily the account of the crucifixion of Jesus from John's Gospel: there were some seventy references to Christ in that Congress. Mrs. Naidu, India's able poetess and Nationalist, sent a poem to the Congress to be read, entitled, "By Love Serve One Another"—a Scripture quotation.

Through the literature and addresses of India's leaders, phrases and sentences from the New Testament run almost like a refrain.

In one of the Provincial Congress addresses Dr. ———, the president, during his address spoke of Mr. C. F. Andrews as "that real Christian," and added, "Would that there were more real Christians!" Incidentally, let it be said that the Hindus often refer to "C. F. A." as standing for "Christ's Faithful Apostle"—a beautiful tribute, and a true one.

In a recent Congress meeting, Mohammed Ali, the leader of the Muslims of India, in his presidential address spoke of Mahatma Gandhi as "that Christlike man." Again and again Hindus rise in my meetings and ask if I do not think that Mahatma Gandhi is a Christlike man. I usually reply that I cordially differ with him in a good many things nevertheless do think in some things he is a very Christlike man indeed. I have had them reply that they would go much further: they believed that he was the incarnation of Christ. A Hindu gave utterance to the same thought when listening to a preacher preaching in the bazaar in North India on the second coming of Christ: "Why do you preach on the second coming of Christ? He has already come—he is here—Gandhi." Blasphemy? That is not the point—the point is that Gandhi is their ideal, and they are identifying that ideal with Jesus. It is the gripping of the mind by the Jesus ideal.

Even the Arya Samaj, which is our bitterest opponent and whose leader said in a recent speech, "You may forget your name, you may forget your mother, but do not forget that the missionaries are the enemies of your country and your civilization"—nevertheless, in a recent editorial in their principal organ, the *Vedic Magazine*, they call Gandhi "This modern Christ." Against the missionary, but unconsciously for his message—Christ!

In an article written by a Hindu in an extreme nationalist paper there occurred this sentence: "Calvary, where another great of the East has suffered martyrdom for the sins of the world, has today its counterpart in Yerravada, where our Mahatmaji suffers martyrdom for the thralldom of the world. Just as Calvary stands for the world sinners, so Yerravada stands for the world's downtrodden." Yerravada is the prison where Gandhi was imprisoned. It is not a question whether these are real parallels or not, the significant thing is that the Indian people are seeing them.

I was talking to two of the followers of Mahatma Gandhi one day when I said, "My brothers, we must have unity between the Hindu and Muslim if our country is ever to be strong and free, but your Hindu-Muslim unity is based upon an incorrect foundation. You have based it upon a religious pact, you should base it upon the unchanging fact that you are all Indians. Upon this basis you should come together. This other will not stand." My Hindu friend replied, "But, Mr. Jones, isn't it our Christian duty to help our Muslim brethren in their difficulties?" A Hindu talking about his Christian duty toward his Muslim brethren!

In the Ashram[2] at Sat Tal the atmosphere is one of beautiful courtesy and friendliness. A Parsee gentleman came into my little room there and placed some flowers on my table. It was a beautiful bit of thoughtfulness. I said, "My brother, that was very gracious of you. I thank you from my heart for that." "Oh, no," he replied, "that was my Christian duty," and then, catching himself, he quickly added, "Yes, and also my Parsee duty." But I wondered if the last portion was not a tribute he felt he must pay to past loyalties, rather like a waving salutation to a dying ideal in his mind? The thing that was gripping him—really gripping him—was that to be kindly and gracious was one's Christian duty while he was still a Parsee—outwardly.

Two of the leaders of India, one in the political and one in the social realm, were talking to a friend of mine when the social leader remarked, "Well, Dr. ———, it is very difficult for us to say where our Hinduism ends and where our Christianity begins!" Turning to the political leader he said,

2. A place of religious retreat.

"Isn't that so, ———?" He pondered a moment and then thoughtfully replied, "Yes, that is so." Our Hinduism ends—our Christianity begins!

At the close of one of my addresses on "Jesus and the Problems of the Day" the Hindu chairman, a prominent social thinker, in his chairman's remarks said, "I suppose that the epitome of what the speaker has said is that the solution of the problems of the day depends upon the application of the mind and spirit of Jesus to those problems. Now, I am not a Christian, and you will be surprised to hear me say that I entirely agree with these conclusions." He went almost immediately from our meeting to be the president of the All-India Social Conference, which deals with the pressing social problems of India's life, and he went there with this underlying thought as to the solution of those problems. Another Hindu chairman put the matter in this way, "The problems of the day arise through the lack of the spirit of Jesus Christ in the affairs of men."

At question time in the sacred city of ———, the editor of the local non-cooperation paper, a brilliant Hindu, a graduate of Oxford University, sent in a long list of keen questions which I was doing my best to answer, when two members of the secret police, the spy-system of India, got up and went behind a pillar and were whispering together and were disturbing him in his listening. These men were no friends of the editor, for they had probably shadowed him quite a bit. To this they were adding this present inconvenience. He twisted in his seat quite a bit and was very ill at ease, and then finally, turning to a friend of mine alongside of him, said, "Mr. J———, I feel most un-Christian toward those men!" Here was a Hindu talking about his un-Christian feelings toward the representatives of a Christian government! Mixed up but illuminating.

In view of the above incidents, and many more like them, I was not surprised to have a Hindu college principal say to me one day, "There is growing up in India a Christ-cult, entirely apart from the Christian Church, almost under its opposition. The leading ideas of that cult are love, service, and self-sacrifice." He did not mean that there was any gathering of this scattered thought into an organization called the Christ-cult. Things are not propagated in India by blocked-off organization as we carry them on in the West. The method of propagation has been by ideas catching from life to life and thus silently leavening the whole. And this permeation that is taking place is running true to the genius of the past, for in the past it was thus that the ideas of the great reformers like Ramanuja and Shankara became dominant. This Christ-cult has become more like an atmosphere than an organization.

But the tremendous question presses itself upon us: Will the present Christian Church be big enough, responsive enough, Christlike enough to be the medium and organ through which Christ will come to India? For, mind you, Christianity is breaking out beyond the borders of the Christian Church. Will the Christian Church be Christlike enough to be the moral and spiritual center of this overflowing Christianity? Or will many of the finest spirits and minds of India accept Christ as Lord and Master of their lives, but live their Christian lives apart from the Christian Church? I believe in the Christian Church with all my heart and believe that in it has centered the finest moral and spiritual life of the world, but here is a new and amazing challenge, for this outside Christianity is going straight to the heart of things and saying that to be a Christian is to be Christlike. This means nothing less than that ancient rituals and orders, and power at court and correctly stated doctrine avail little if Christlikeness is not the outstanding characteristic of the life of the people of the churches. If Christianity centers in the Christian Church in the future, it will be because that church is the center of the Christ-spirit. This constitutes a challenge and a call.

This whole chapter might be summed up in the statement of the Brahman who put his hand on my shoulder (and I am untouchable!) and said, "Sir, you perhaps become discouraged at the few who become Christians from the high castes. You need not be discouraged. You do not know how far your gospel has gone. Now, look at me. I am a Brahman, but I would call myself a Christian Brahman, for I am trying to live my life upon the principles and spirit of Jesus, though I may never come out and be an open follower of Jesus Christ, but I am following him. Sir, don't be discouraged, you do not know how far your gospel has gone."

I was not discouraged, my heart was singing to the music of things, for I saw my risen Lord entering behind closed doors once again and showing his hands and his side and speaking peace to disciples I had not known.

As the physical atmosphere becomes heavy with moisture, so heavy that it is precipitated into rain, so the spiritual atmosphere of India is becoming heavy with interest in Jesus Christ and is on the verge of and is actually being precipitated into Christian forms and Christian expression. I pray that the Christian Church may be the Christlike medium through which this spiritual precipitation may express itself.

But one word of caution before closing this chapter. Do not misunderstand me. I am not satisfied with an interest in Jesus—I cannot be satisfied this side of allegiance—utter and absolute. But if you give me an inch in the soul of India, I will take it and appeal for that next inch until the whole soul of this great people is laid at the feet of the Son of God.

Moreover, our final call to the world is not to love Christ, but to have faith in him. But since a nation is gradually won, we will thank God for any stage on the way to the goal we can find. That final goal is faith in Christ.

But He who was grateful for the cup of cold water given in his name, who accepted the superstitious touch of a woman upon the border of his garment and let healing flow through that imperfect touch, who rejoiced in the faith of an outsider and said that he had not found so great faith in Israel, and gave him his heart's desire, who would not break the bruised reed or quench the smoking flax, who saw in a grateful woman's anointing of his feet a meaning deeper than she saw, declaring it to have significance for his burial, who caught and responded to the cry of a penitent thief for remembrance, certainly will not despise this day of small but prophetic beginnings and will bring these "other sheep who are not of this fold, that there may be one flock [R. V.] and one shepherd" (John 10:16).[3]

3. Jones's bracketed note indicates he is relying on the Revised Version of the King James Bible for some of the wording here.

CHAPTER IV

JESUS COMES THROUGH IRREGULAR CHANNELS—MAHATMA GANDHI'S PART

WHILE a Christian lecturer was commenting on this remarkable permeation of the atmosphere of India with the thought and spirit of Jesus, a Hindu turned and said to me, "Yes, but he failed to say that Mahatma Gandhi was responsible for a great deal of this new interest in Jesus." I could only agree with him that the criticism was just.

Mahatma Gandhi does not call himself a Christian. The fact is that he calls himself a Hindu. But by his life and outlook and methods he has been the medium through which a great deal of this interest in Christ has come.

He saw clearly that there were two ways that India might gain her freedom. She might take the way of the sword and the bomb—the way that Mohammed Ali and Shankat Ali, the Muslim leaders, untamed by Gandhi, would have taken; and the way that the Bengal anarchists have actually taken. The fires of rebellion were underneath. The flash of a bomb here and there let the world see in that lurid light what was there. Gandhi brought all this hidden discontent to the open. A member of the secret police told me that it was comparatively easy for them now since Gandhi's advent, that they simply went to the Non-Cooperation Headquarters and asked what the next step in their program in the fight with the government would be and they told him just what they would do next. Gandhi turned the streams of discontent and rebellion into open and frank channels.

He rejected both the sword and the bomb, not because it was expedient, but because he believed with all his soul in something else, in another type of power—soul force or the power of suffering—and another type of victory—a victory over oneself, this inward victory being the precursor of the outward national victory. In the fires of that suffering there would come the inward freedom, the purification of the social and political life from within.

Now for the first time in human history a nation in the attainment of its national ends repudiated physical force and substituted the power of soul or soul force and has made inward national regeneration a vital part of its program. This is certainly an infinitely more Christian way than we have ordinarily taken in the West. Had the Indian people really caught the ideal on a national scale and put it into practice, as an inner circle caught and practiced it, they would have risen to almost unparalleled moral heights. As one English writer, who is not supposed to be sympathetic, put it, "Had India really practiced Gandhi's program, no nation on earth could have denied to India the moral leadership of the world." They would have shown us a way out of the vicious circle into which militarism has got us. They would have demonstrated what we all vaguely feel, that the final power of the world resides in soul.

The daily Anglo-Indian paper, the *Statesman*, after bitterly fighting Gandhi and his movement, acknowledged in its editorial columns that Gandhi "had put sincerity into politics." He did more: he put the cross into politics.

The movement as a political movement failed, for violence crept into it. The movement failed, but it was not a failure. The immediate end was not accomplished, but it left a spiritual deposit in the mind of India that will never be lost.

At the close of an address on "Gandhi" in America a man arose and asked why I talked on Gandhi and his movement when both of them were abject failures. I replied that I did so because I belonged to that other and greater Failure of human history—to the Man who began a kingdom with initial success and then it all ended in a cross, a bitter and shameful Failure. But Golgotha's failure was the world's most amazing success. A recent dramatist made the centurion say to Mary as she stood by the cross: "I tell you, woman, that this dead Son of yours, disfigured, shamed, spat upon, has built a kingdom this day that can never die. The living glory of him rules it. The earth is *his* and he made it. He and his brothers have been molding and making it through the long ages; they are the only ones who ever did possess it; not the proud, not the idle, not the vaunting empires of the world. Something has happened up here on this hill today to shake all the kingdoms of blood and fear to dust. The earth is his, the earth is theirs, and they made it. The meek, the terrible meek, the fierce agonizing meek, are about to enter into their inheritance."[1] If the meek shall finally inherit earth, then Gandhi must get his portion, for he belongs to the meek, the terrible meek.

Do not misunderstand me, I do not draw the parallels, thereby suggesting that these events are comparable in their effect upon human history but belonging to the Great Failure that meant world redemption, I am predisposed to understand a failure that may mean something bigger than political success for India—and beyond.

Gandhi did not fail. The Indian people failed Gandhi. It was their failure. But in apparent failure he really succeeded. I would rather think of him as Gandhi the defeated, but holding

1. Charles Rann Kennedy, *The Terrible Meek* (New York: Harper & Brothers, 1912), 39.

firm and with fresh spirit to the belief that somehow, someway the power of his ideal must conquer, than to see Gandhi seated by some other method as the first president of the Indian Republic. We have plenty of presidents throughout the world. We have a new crop every election day. China has one every few months by the clicking of political and military machinery, but few outside China know their names; but the name of Gandhi haunts us, shocks us, appeals to us. If Gandhi should die right now in the moment of his most apparent failure, disagree with him as I do in many things, I would hold him to be the most successful man who has lived in East or West in the last ten years. I think history will bear that out. I would rather be a Woodrow Wilson, or a Gandhi defeated, but holding to ideals not yet accepted, than to be a Clemenceau, the tiger, standing victorious over a fallen foe.

Gandhi's movement in its failure left a new spiritual deposit in the mind of India. The cross has become intelligible and vital. Up to a few years ago one was preaching against a stone wall in preaching the cross in India. The whole underlying philosophy of things was against it. The doctrine of karma, as ordinarily held, has little or no room for the cross in it. According to it, you are being meted out, to the last jot and tittle, the results of your actions in a previous birth. Everything is held in the iron grip of that law of rewards and punishments. If you help a man, it is because his Karma calls for that help; if you hurt him, it is for the same reason. All suffering is punitive and the result of previous sin. This thought prompted a man to ask me in one of my meetings "if Jesus must not have been a very wicked man in a previous birth, since he was such a terrible sufferer in this one." This was a view consistent with the doctrine. There is little or no room for vicarious suffering for others.

But with this teaching of Gandhi that they can joyously take on themselves suffering for the sake of national ends, there has come into the atmosphere a new sensitivity to the cross. A brilliant Hindu thinker, writing on this subject, said, "What the missionaries have not been able to do in fifty years Gandhi by his life and trial and incarceration has done, namely, he has turned the eyes of India toward the cross." I am a missionary, and you would expect that comment to make us missionaries wince a bit, but it does not. We do not mind who gets the credit. We are not there for credit, but for reality. We desire so desperately that India and the world may see the cross that we rejoice if anyone, even one outside our fold, helps India see that cross. Today in India you can step up from this nationalist thinking straight to the heart of the cross. It is the message that goes through with power.

Even a Muslim editor caught the inner meaning of things—and it is difficult for Muslims who have other ideas of power—and expressed it in an editorial thus: "From the mere standpoint of strategy it is infinitely better for the missionaries to depend upon the cross and its meaning of self-sacrifice than upon all the empires and their backing."

This little window lets us see a good deal: In a Nationalist paper at the time of great national excitement there appeared this flaming headline, "A Dreadful Night of Crucifixion." I read through the account with eagerness to see what had happened. It was a vivid account of how Akali Sikhs, resisters, were severely beaten by the police. It ended with this sentence: "Gentle reader, on that dreadful night Christ was again crucified." This was written by a Hindu for Hindus and Muslims, but they had caught the idea that Christ was identified in some mysterious way with the pain and suffering and oppression of humanity. Whether the text taken will bear the burden of the meaning given to it is not the question; the idea lives on even after the event to which it is applied passes away. That idea is that Christ suffers in the suffering of humanity.

A nationalist put the matter to me this way: "It is you Christians who can understand the inner meaning of our movement better than others, for it has a kinship to the underlying thought of Christianity." The man who said this was a man of beautiful character and was acting upon that inner meaning. One nationalist asked me, "Do you not think that the Non-Cooperation movement is an application of the principles of Jesus to the present political situation?"

Some of the Hindus have been concerned about this too definitely Christian aspect of things. One of them asked in my meeting, "Just as the British government conquered India through the sons of the soil, that is, through Indian troops, aren't you trying to conquer India for Christianity in the same way, namely, by using a son of the soil, Gandhi?" Of course, this was preposterous, for Gandhi is the last man on earth who can be "handled"; but the point is that the questioner saw the Christian drift of things.

In one of the important conferences when the nationalist leaders were discussing this question of procedure a Hindu nationalist said, "I oppose this non-violent non-cooperation. I ask you is it Hindu teaching? It is not. Is it an Islamic teaching? It is not. I will tell you what it is, it is Christian teaching. I therefore oppose it."

Even among the ordinary villagers this drift is noted. At ——— the missionaries had been bitterly opposed by the Hindus in their preaching at a mela, a religious fair. But this year of which I speak the Hindus came and helped them, saying, "We are allies now, since Mahatma Gandhi is following Christ." The question of whether he would say he is or not is not the paramount thing—the point is that the villagers saw the inner relationship of things.

This viewpoint of the villagers is not to be wondered at when an instance like this occurs: On the arrival of the train the great crowd gathered for a speech. Gandhi came out, took out a New Testament and read the Beatitudes and then finished by saying: "That is my address to you. Act upon that." That was all the speech he gave. But it spoke volumes.

In one place the nationalists were forbidden by the government to carry the national flag beyond a certain point on a bridge which led into the European or Civil section of the town. The nationalists made it an issue. The magistrate, who arrested and tried most of them, remarked to me that those whom he arrested were much more Christian in their spirit than he was. They would let him know what time they were coming across the bridge with the flag and how many! Would he please be prepared for twenty-five today. Of the twelve hundred who were arrested in that flag agitation, although none of them were professed Christians, and although they could take into jail with them only a limited number of things which they had to produce before the magistrate, the vast majority took New Testaments with them to read while there. The reason they did so becomes apparent when one of them remarked, "We now know what it means for you Christians to suffer for Christ." The cross had become not a doctrine, but a living thing to them.

Sometimes things took a rather amusing if not ludicrous turn, as when a Hindu nationalist who was being tried by a British judge began his defense with these words, "And they shall deliver you up before kings and governors and magistrates for my name's sake," and ended up his statement with the words, "Father, forgive them, they know not what they do!"

But the real force of it strikes one when Gandhi himself exemplifies it. He is ready to apply this principle of conquering by soul force not merely against the British government, but against his own people as well, when he feels they are in the wrong. This, of course, would have little or no effect were not Gandhi the soul of sincerity and utterly fearless.

When in South Africa carrying on his passive resistance movement against the South African government (which struggle, by the way, he won) the indentured laborers in whose behalf he was fighting with non-violent weapons, got out of hand again and again. He remonstrated, but all to no avail. Finally, without a word he went off and began to fast. He had fasted for two days when word went around among the laborers that Gandhi was fasting because of what they were doing. That changed matters immediately. They came to him with folded hands and begged him to desist from the fast, promising him that they would do anything if only he would stop it. Suffering love had conquered.

In his ashram one of the boys told him something that he believed but later found out that the boy had lied to him. Gandhi called the school together and solemnly said, "Boys, I am sorry to find out that one of you is a liar. As punishment I am going off and fast today." That may be passed with a smile, but not if you knew the dead earnestness of Gandhi and the sheer moral weight of the man. There could not have been a more terrific punishment, for long after any physical pain from physical punishment would have died away there would persist the spiritual pain from the lashings of conscience awakened by the sufferings of the man who loved him. In the light of Gandhi's acting thus, it becomes easy for them to step up from the thought that if one man would take on himself suffering to bring a boy back from a lie to the truth, then if there were One divine enough and holy enough, he might take on his soul the very sin of a whole race to bring us back to good and to God. The cross thus bursts into meaning when lighted up by this lesser act.

This is all the more vividly seen in Gandhi's recent fast of twenty-one days. A fast of that length of time is serious when we recall that Gandhi had not really recovered from his operation and that he ordinarily weighs less than a hundred pounds. But when he came out of jail, he found the Hindus and Muslims suspicious, jealous, and divided. Before his arrest they had become united in his person, but when he was taken away and put in jail they fell apart. He knew that the moment India was united, that moment India was free. He pleaded and remonstrated, but the divisions persisted and became acute. Out of sheer sorrow of heart he announced that he would undergo, as a penance, a fast of twenty-one days.

It touched India to the quick, for they are an emotionally responsive people. They called a Unity Conference on the tenth day of his fast. It was composed of representatives of the various religions of India, including the Metropolitan, the head of the Church of England in India. They debated back and forth the questions at issue. Though Gandhi was lying in weakness upon his couch in another part of the city, his spirit pressed upon them in the conference for a solution. They passed resolutions covering their points of difference and appointed a commission of twenty-five as a Permanent Board of Adjudication on intercommunal matters. But the most remarkable resolution was the one in which they stated that "We recognize the right of an individual to change his faith at will, provided no inducement is offered to effect that change, such as the offering of material gain," and, further, "We also recognize the right of that individual not to suffer persecution from the community which he may leave." When one remembers that in Islam apostasy meant death, and in Hinduism social death, then this resolution marks a national epoch and is really a National Declaration of Religious Freedom. The silent pressure of the spirit of Gandhi was doing its work. And Gandhi's spirit was being pressed upon by the Spirit of Jesus.

On the eighteenth day of the fast, Mr. C. F. Andrews, who was editing Gandhi's paper, *Young India*, while he was fasting, wrote an editorial in which he described Gandhi lying upon his couch on the upper veranda in Delhi, weak and emaciated. He pictured the fort which could be seen in the distance, reminding them of the struggle for the possession of the kingdom; below the fort Englishmen could be seen going out to their golf; nearer at hand the crowds of his own people surged through the bazaar intent on buying and selling. While Andrews watched him there that verse of Scripture rushed to his mind: "Is it nothing to you, ye that pass by? Is there any sorrow like unto my sorrow?" (Lamentations 1:12). He ended it with this sentence: "As I looked upon him there and caught the meaning of it all, I felt as never before in my own experience the meaning of the cross."

Andrews spoke out in these last sentences the very thought of the heart of India. India has seen the meaning of the cross in one of her sons. As a former fiery opponent of Christianity, a nationalist leader, said, "I never understood the meaning of Christianity until I saw it in Gandhi." While this inspires us and we are deeply grateful for it, nevertheless, it is a sword that cuts two ways, for some of us have been there these years and deeply regret that Christianity did not burst into meaning through us. However, we are glad that India is seeing. And let it be quietly said that we too are seeing.

CHAPTER V

Through the Regular Channels—Some Evangelistic Series

THE picture given in the preceding chapter must be corrected a bit, for while Gandhi has had a good deal to do with popularizing the latent sentiment lying in the soul of India, nevertheless it has been the missionaries and their associates who through these decades have, by their fine living and self-sacrifice and constant teaching, laid up this sentiment in the heart of India. I have constantly felt my own debt of gratitude as I have gone from place to place entering into other people's labors. They sowed where I was privileged to reap. It was they who have had the harder part.

Some time ago I got hold of a phrase that has been of incalculable value to me: "Evangelize the inevitable." Certain things are inevitable: no use to grumble against them—get into them and evangelize them. The labor movement throughout the world is inevitable. In England they more or less evangelized the movement so that it is very Christian in its spirit and outlook. We failed to do that in America so that the movement sometimes fell into the hands of men who were anti-Christian. This has been of incalculable loss. Some years ago, I saw that the Nationalist Movement in India was inevitable.

You could not scatter as much education and Christian teaching through India without there being an uprising of soul demanding self-expression and self-control. It is as inevitable as the dawn. We would have felt that we had failed if this had not come. When I saw the inevitableness of it, I felt there was only one thing to be done—get into the movement and evangelize it. Stand down in those national currents and put Christ there.

That does not mean that we should get into the politics of the country and become politicians, but it does mean that the Indian Nationalist senses at once that we are in spiritual sympathy with the finest and best in his movement. That is all he asks for, but he does ask for that.

When I began this work nine years ago it was, in a small way, hoping that this most difficult field would open. I have had no plans that I was not ready to scrap, if they did not seem to be vital or did not work. There was one concern and one only: how could I help India to see in Jesus what I saw. Anything that ministered to that I wanted, anything that did not could go.

Since the Methodist Board took charge of my expenses and then gave me perfect freedom to work among all the different missions of India, I have covered several times the more important centers and many smaller ones.

We have had as chairmen of our meetings members of Legislative Councils, judges, lawyers, generals, college presidents, professors, and leading Hindus and Muslims of every type. We have had the meetings in the open spaces in the cool of the evenings, in Town Halls, Hindu and Christian college auditoriums, Theosophical Society halls and even in Hindu temple compounds. The reader will probably note that I have omitted Christian churches from this list. There is a real prejudice against them, so we seldom or never have meetings for Hindus and Muslims in them.

We have felt that we must hit the problem in two places: The church must be spiritualized and the non-Christian won to Christ. We have morning meetings for the Christians and night meetings for the non-Christians. These are tied together in purpose, for we know that we cannot spiritualize the church apart from its tasks. Experience and expression are the two sides of the Christian life, and one cannot exist without the other. Kill either and you kill both. So, we have tried to get the church to realize its joyous privilege of soul-winning.

One task along this line has been to help arouse the Syrian Church in South India—a church of five hundred thousand that has been dead for centuries. They are now beginning to be keen and alive, and the largest Christian audience in the world gathers at the time of their yearly convention, when in a single audience there will be thirty-five thousand people. These conventions have been marked with great spiritual power, and the church is now beginning to take its place in the evangelization of India.[1]

In the meetings for non-Christians there have been large crowds in many places, and although it has been the most upset period of India's recent history, yet we have not had the slightest disturbance of any kind in any single meeting in nine years. India has shown a beautiful courtesy and has treated me as a friend and brother, and I have tried to respond in kind.

I said there had been no disturbance, but there was one on one occasion, but that was based on a misunderstanding. The Non-Cooperators, the extreme Nationalists, saw the officials of the city going into our meeting and thought we were having a pro-government meeting. They surrounded the building, stoned it, rushed to the doors, and yelled their national yells for three quarters of an hour. I requested some men to hold the

1. The Maramon Convention, which E. Stanley Jones attended for years as a speaker, still continues today and is held each February on the same riverbank.

doors, and above the din and noise I talked on brotherhood and good will and the coming of the Kingdom, while the storm raged on the outside. It was a lovely time to talk about it! But the next day when the Non-Cooperators found out what kind of a meeting we were having they came and personally apologized and said that they themselves would attend the rest of the meetings. They did so, and one of them, on the last night of the meeting, dressed in his simple white homespun, the sign of the Nationalist, arose and read a paper thanking me for what I had said to them about Christ. That was the nearest to a disturbance we had had in nine years. The gentle courtesy of the East is a beautiful thing. For instance, after speaking for a number of nights in a Theosophical Society Hall it was a fine courtesy for the secretary of the Society to garland me publicly, though everything I had said cut straight across the ideas of theosophy.

In view of what I have said above, the criticism of Bernard Lucas, author of *Christ for India*, is just when he remarks, "We have attempted the task of winning India for Christ as though it were a country of barbarians, whereas it is a country of cultured and civilized people with a submerged tenth of barbarians." It is usually about that submerged tenth that we hear in our general missionary talks, which taken alone can hardly be called a fair representation of the situation. At the same time, I realize that my presentation needs the balance of the other facts.

I know when I stand before an audience of Hindus and Muslims that they are inwardly challenging every word I utter and every thought I express; and I know if I gain an inch in their souls, I will have to fight for it, but all the time there is courtesy and friendliness, even in moments of deepest disagreement. Such treatment can fairly be claimed to indicate culture.

Now for a few glimpses into some of the evangelistic series. I select these out of the hundreds we have had throughout India.

We went into the great city of ———. It was an exceedingly difficult proposition, for there was a great university there which was supposed to propagate Hindu culture and religion. On the other hand, the city was held in the grip of ancient thought and many a superstition. But we were amazed and delighted to find that the president of the university graciously consented to become chairman of one of our meetings. There were large crowds each night. At the close of the meeting one night the students of the university came and asked me to come over to speak at the university. I was surprised beyond measure and said, "My brothers, you don't want me over there?"

"Oh, yes, we do," they replied.

But I pressed a little further: "Do your professors know about it?" "Yes," they said, "they want you to come."

"But," I still persisted, "what do you want me to speak about?"

One of them answered and said, "If you don't mind, we would like you to speak about Christ."

Well, I assure you, I didn't mind!

Another spoke up and said, "We would like you to speak especially about the cross." I like to speak especially about the cross! I went over several times, and on the first occasion was introduced by the Hindu chairman, a professor, in these words. "I have been attending the public meetings, but I haven't been interested in the speaker as much as I have been interested in the Person concerning whom he has been speaking. Young men, no such personality as that of Jesus has ever appeared in human history. He is the greatest character that has ever been in our world. Now, today is a Hindu festival, and we can begin the festival in no better way than to hear again about this Person." The striking thing was that I could see no sign of resentment on the faces of the students. Knowing the bitterness and prejudices of the past, I could scarcely believe my ears, for we were at the heart of orthodoxy.

In the same place I was invited by the Theosophists to speak to them in their hall. At the close their leader said, "We may not agree with what Mr. Jones is saying, but we can certainly all try to be like Jesus Christ"—which is a good deal!

In ——— the meetings were in the Town Hall. The next to the last night of the series, the leaders of the Non-Cooperation movement in that place publicly presented a request at the close. They said that the next day was the anniversary of Mahatma Gandhi's going to jail and it was their big day, that they were going to have a great meeting of ten thousand or more on the public commons, and they had come to ask us to put these two meetings together. They asked me to speak on the same topic announced for that next night and said they would furnish an interpreter. I strongly desired to go, for it was such a gracious invitation and meant so much, for it was their greatest political gathering and they wanted me to give a Christian address! But the next night I wanted to give an invitation for personal allegiance to Christ. Very reluctantly I had to decline their invitation. Notwithstanding the fact that the other meeting was going on at the same time, our meeting was packed to its capacity. At the close of the address, I did what I have only dared to do this last year. I asked these leading high-caste men to take their stand publicly for Christ. I told them frankly that I would leave the question of baptism and the Christian Church to their consciences, that I would give them my own view, namely, that I believed that inwardly and outwardly one should belong to Christ, but, having said that, I would leave the matter to their consciences as they read the New Testament, and in its light decided what they should do. But I urged that here and now they should make Jesus the Lord and Savior of their lives. On that proposition, between thirty and forty of the leading citizens, lawyers, doctors, and so on, stayed. That aftermeeting in which we prayed and instructed them and had them repeat a prayer of confession and surrender to Christ was one long to be remembered, for the melting sense of God that was upon us.

We have had some of our meetings in some very remarkable places. In ——— we had them in the palace of Tippu Sultan, the old Muslim king and tyrant. I stood right under the throne when I spoke. It made a splendid sounding board in more ways than one. The last night, I asked those who would give themselves to Christ to meet me in a little room in the rear. It filled up with seeking Hindus—some of them in earnest—a few who had come to challenge and quibble. I found out later that the room was the place where two British generals had been chained to their guards as prisoners of the tyrant. One of them was named Sir David Baird. When word went to his old mother in Scotland about her son, the dour old lady, knowing her boy, said, "Well, God have mercy on the poor chap that is chained to our Davy!" But in the very room where men had been chained to their guards as prisoners, Christ was making men free, and in the palace hall where an autocrat had sat with a kingdom founded upon a bloody sword, we were announcing a new kingdom founded not upon the sword, but upon the very self-giving of the Son of God at Golgotha.

At one place, a non-Christian literary society asked to have the meetings under their auspices and charge. A non-Christian literary society having charge of Christian evangelistic meetings! Incongruous, but glorious! They secured the Maharaja's theater for the addresses. They said they were going to get the prince as the chairman of the meeting the first night. They naïvely suggested that he was hard hit by drink, but they thought they could keep him sufficiently sober to be chairman that night! We cannot be squeamish about those things, we have to take what we get, glad to put out our gospel in any situation we can, and since we thought the prince needed it, we were very glad to have him come. The prime minister was the chairman the second night and on down the line to lesser officials. There were about a thousand of the officials of that leading native state present each night. It was literally like witnessing before kings and governors for His name's sake. When the prince arose for his chairman's remarks, everyone was rather nervous as to what he would say, for he was rather a freelance speaker and said about what he wanted to say. He kept up his reputation for surprises by saying, "I do not understand why the speaker has gone so far off to talk about corruption in government; he needn't have gone to China to talk about corrupt officials; he could have come right here." Every official jumped as though he had been shot. Just then his secretary, who was an influential man in the state and who was on the platform with us, hurriedly passed over a note to the prince. He read it and then announced, "My secretary says I need not say anything more!"

He invited me to come over to see him at the palace the next day. I went. I begged him to give up drink and give himself to Christ, told him what Christ had done for me. He said, "Mr. Jones, I can't do it. The fact is that I was almost a Christian when I first went to England, for Christianity appealed to me because of its sense of brotherhood; but I was educated there with a book by Thomas Babington Macaulay in one hand and a whisky bottle in the other. But I will make you this promise. I am going to America, and since you have prohibition in America, I won't be able to get it then, so I will give it up when I go there." The whole world is bending over in expectancy to see what we are going to do with this matter of prohibition. If we should fail, it would set back the clock of moral progress for fifty or a hundred years. We must not fail. Thus does evangelistic work in Asia depend upon conditions at home.

Nine years ago, Dr. John R. Mott was speaking in the fine hall at ——— to a non-Christian audience. In the midst of his address, he used the name of Christ, and the audience hissed him. Nine years later, we were in that hall with one topic for six nights—"Jesus Christ and Him Crucified." The audience increased every night until the last night they were standing around the doors and windows. I gave the invitation to those who would surrender themselves to Christ, leaving the question of baptism to their own inner convictions, to come and take the front seats. I felt at the time that if one would come, I should be grateful, for William Carey had said that if one of these high castes should ever be converted, it would be as great a miracle as the raising of the dead. But that night between a hundred and a hundred and fifty came forward on that proposal. Cut it down to its lowest possible significance, and yet we have left the residual fact that in the hall where the name of Christ had been hissed nine years before, men now stayed to pray in that same name. It was not the difference in the speakers, for everything was in favor of the first speaker; it was the difference in the attitude of India toward Jesus in the meantime. "The psychological climate" has changed. It was a new day.

In this same city I was invited to speak in a non-Christian college, and the students gave up a cricket match in order to attend. In another place the Hindu students wanted an extra meeting for themselves. We could find no time, for I was speaking four times a day. They decided to have it at seven o'clock in the morning. The theme was "How to Find a New Life!"

The Hindu clerks of a certain city wanted an extra meeting, and since no other time could be found, they came out at 7:30 a.m. before going to their offices.

The Non-Cooperators had captured the municipality of ——— and were in charge. The whole city was dressed in white home-spun khaddar, the sign of the Nationalist. When one went into the city with other than white garments on, he felt like a speckled bird. Riots had taken place nearby, and feelings were running very high. The British official in charge of the district warned us that if we went into the city for meetings, he could not be responsible for our safety. But we felt we should go and went. One of the missionaries wrote to Mr. Gandhi and told him that I was giving addresses in the city and asked him to kindly write to his Nationalists and ask them to come. He wrote back immediately, for he is very prompt in his correspondence, and said that we would be very happy to have his people come, in fact, had written them to that effect. When they got this word, they came to us and asked if they could not take charge of the meetings. I told them that I was not going to talk politics, but Christ. Nevertheless, three of the leading Hindu Nationalists signed the notices that went out calling the meetings. The hall filled up immediately, so we had to go out into the open air. I saw at once that a good many of my listeners did not understand English. Let me say parenthetically that I speak almost entirely in English to these non-Christian audiences, for nearly all the intelligentsia know English, since the medium of instruction in the high schools and colleges is English. Sometimes, you can use the best you have, and it is none too good. I saw at a glance that some of my audience was not English educated. I turned to my chairman and said, "I am not sure what I should do, for I do not know Gujarati [that was the local language]. I only know Hindustani, and there is no Christian here to interpret for me." He promptly replied, "I shall be very happy indeed to interpret for you if you like." Here was a very long cry from the expectation of suffering violence at their hands, as the official had feared, to their taking charge of our meetings and interpreting our message! I wondered how I would get my Christian message through my Hindu brother, but I remembered that David Brainerd (1718–1747) used to preach through drunken interpreters to the American Indians and the power of the Spirit rested upon the meetings in spite of this, and I believed God would do the same thing for us as our fine Hindu friend interpreted our message. And he did!

The next night they gave me another interpreter, also a Hindu, and we gave the message of the cross through him.

At the close of the meeting one night, I asked if they would like me to pray. I never pray publicly without asking their permission, and I have never had them refuse. At the close of the prayer a Muslim gentleman came up to me and said, "That was very disrespectful tonight—you had those people sit down while they prayed. They should have stood up in the presence of God!"

"All right," I replied, "tomorrow night they will stand up."

When I finished the next night, I again asked if they would like me to pray. They assented, so I asked them to rise. Now, it was the custom there that whenever they rose for the close of a meeting they always gave their national yells, so when they rose for the prayer across the audience went tremendous waves of "Vande Mataram" and "Mahatma Gandhi ki jai"—"Hail to the Motherland" and "Hail to Mahatma Gandhi!" Between my evangelistic appeal and my prayer, we had the national cries. A glorious mixture! Somehow it didn't jar, and when it quieted a bit I went on with my prayer as though nothing had happened. But India is nothing unless she is mixed—she mingles life and religion in a glorious confusion. I rather like it so!

At the close of the meeting, I suggested that I could not get close enough to them in these big meetings and asked if we might have a Round Table Conference with the leading citizens of this city. They assented, so the next day we met in the national school. I put off my shoes to the side and sat among them on the floor in pandit style. I saw that some of them had been parading the public streets, for they had placards on themselves on which was written:

"Don't pay your taxes to this Government."

"Go to jail with joy."

"The tears of the weak will undermine the strongest wall."

One would have thought that in an atmosphere of this kind, with the whole thing nervous with national excitement, there would be no spiritual response to my message. Here was a real struggle going on. Would they respond at all? On the contrary, there was a fine spiritual sensitiveness. Incidentally, may I say that I have been struck very forcibly with the difference in what happens to the spiritual natures of men who are engaged in warfare with military arms, and those with weapons of non-violent passive resistance. While there are many notable and noble exceptions, it is a truism to say that in war carried on by physical arms, the men who are engaged in it are brutalized—the more so, the more efficient. On the contrary, I have found that the men who threw themselves in with Gandhi and really practiced his program were spiritualized; it deepened their sense of moral values and made them self-sacrificial. Nothing could be a greater condemnation of the one type and a commendation of the other than the respective effects upon the personalities engaged in them. Here I sat before men—very determined men—who were willing to lose their all in the fight they were making with a system of government from the West to which I belonged, and there was no hatred, only a heightened moral and spiritual appreciation and sensitiveness.

I talked to them of my Master. In the midst of the discussion, I used the phrase the "Christ of the Indian Road" and I noted how they kept referring to it again and again. It had caught their imagination. He seemed so intimately theirs. Jesus seemed to have come in from the Indian Road and had sat upon the floor with us there in the quietness of that Indian twilight. In the discussion we talked of India and her need. I did not talk to them as though India were foreign to me, for it was no longer so. I was born in the West and love it, but India has become my home; India's people have become my people; her problems, my problems; her future, my future; and

I would like to wear upon my heart her sins if I could lift her to my Savior. I told them I wanted to be thought of as at least an adopted son of India. I turned to them and said: "Brothers, what can we do with these sixty million outcastes? They are a millstone around our national neck. Our country will never be strong until we lift them. How can we do it?"

A thoughtful Hindu rose and said, "It will take a Christ to lift them."

As we sat there in the soft light of that Indian evening every one of us felt that he was right. It *would* take a Christ to lift them. But some of us went further and included ourselves in it—it would take a Christ to lift us too, and not all of those who felt this way were avowed followers of this Christ.

The Indian people are an intensely religious people, and when the wealth of this wonderful spiritual capacity is placed at the disposal of Jesus the product will be beautiful indeed. One day some prominent Hindus came to me and said, "They are having a government fair at K———." (It was very like our county fair at home with exhibits, agricultural displays, horse racing, sports, wrestling, etc.) "It is all very good, but there is no religion in it. We have come to ask if you won't come and put some religion in it." I asked what they would like me to do, and they replied, "We want you to come and give some addresses in the Durbar Tent." I gasped, for the Durbar Tent was the official tent where the government officials held their functions. I told them to go and see if they could secure the Durbar Tent. They returned indignant. "The idea," they said, "the official said to us that we could not have the addresses in the Durbar Tent, for that would seem to imply that government was back of religion, but we could have them in the wrestling pit with its tiers of seats all around. The idea of putting religion into the wrestling pit! If we can't put it in the Durbar Tent, we won't have the meeting at all!" We had no meetings. But I had the feeling as I talked with those men that when India really accepts Christ he will not be put off on the edges of life. He will be put at the very seat of government to control and mold and possess all.

The last night I was in India before sailing to America for my current furlough I was addressing an eager crowd of non-Christians in ——. It was the last night of the series, and the situation became tense and electric as I asked them to then and there make a personal decision for Christ. I was in the midst of my appeal when a Hindu suddenly stopped me and said: "Wait a minute, sir, you ask us to become Christians. Before you go on will you tell me what you are doing in regard to the question of the rights of Indians in America? Tell us that before you ask us to follow Christ." I was compelled to stop and explain just my position in the matter; told him how some of us had signed a protest to the Department of State among other things. He seemed satisfied but note this: before I could go on and finish up my appeal, I had to make myself right on that whole racial situation. I could not advance another inch without that.

You can see from these little windows I have thrown open what an amazing evangelistic opportunity presents itself. There has never been anything so big and challenging. But we cannot advance into it, cannot handle it with any degree of moral and spiritual authority, until we right ourselves upon some of these great racial issues.

That leads me to my next chapter, a chapter which I dislike to face, but the whole program of the evangelization of the East depends upon our taking a Christian attitude toward the nations of Asia.

CHAPTER VI

THE GREAT HINDRANCE

TO understand the attitude of India toward the West one has to keep in mind the existence in India of what Professor H. A. Miller calls "an oppression psychosis." He defines "oppression" as "the domination of one group by another, politically, economically, or culturally, singly or in combination." And by "psychosis" he means "those persistent and aggravated mental conditions which are characteristically produced under conditions where one group dominates another."[1] India feels that she is being dominated culturally, economically, and politically by the West. An "oppression psychosis" has resulted.

A good deal of the bitter criticism of the West on the part of India at the present time is undoubtedly the result of that psychosis. Under existing conditions, it is almost psychologically impossible for India to find or appreciate any good in the West and openly acknowledge it. Indians may appropriate from the West, but as long as they are conscious that they are Indians they cannot acknowledge their debt. I have found many foreign students in America who were getting all their education and training here, but I have not seen a single one who, while being self-conscious as an Indian, could find anything good in America or her civilization. Only at times when they, for

1. Herbert Adolphus Miller, "The Oppression Psychosis and the Immigrant," *The Annals of the American Academy of Political and Social Science* 93 (January 1921), 139.

the moment, forgot they were Indians could they acknowledge any good.

I do not think that India will ever openly and frankly appropriate from Western civilization or from the Western church until she is freed from this oppression psychosis, in other words, till she is politically self-governing.

Britain has on the whole given India good government, but until India feels she stands as a free people there can be no frank and balanced evaluation of what the West contains.

India can now take from Christ because she is able to disassociate him from the West, but she finds it difficult to take from the Christian Church or from missionaries, for in these cases the disassociation is not easy. But even here missionaries may lose their Western identity, so to speak, and may so merge their lives and endeavors with India that they are no longer a part of the dominating influences but take their place as serving friends and brothers. As a social thinker, a Hindu, said to me, "Western civilization was never at such a low ebb in our estimate as now, but you missionaries never stood higher; you come not to exploit us but to serve us." If we come as the servants of the situation, we step out of any dominating movement that may be the program of the West.

In dealing with the criticism of India toward the West we must keep in mind this psychosis, make allowances for it, and be patient.

But we fool ourselves if we dismiss it at that. For this oppression psychosis has very good basis for its existence—not so much from deliberate governmental policy as from the daily contacts of white men with brown persons; the snobbery, the taken-for-granted attitude that any white man is superior to any brown man—these are the things that rub into soreness the soul of India and make it smart. If the Indian, smarting under these assumed attitudes, turns upon the West in invective and biting criticism, let us remember that his criticism is pointed with the knowledge the Indian now possesses that when we take these attitudes, we are cutting absolutely across everything that our religion teaches. He knows that these things are not Christian.

If the centering of everything upon the person of Jesus clears the issue and has given us a new vitalizing of our work in India, nevertheless it has come back upon us in a terrific judgment. India is doing nothing less than judging us in the light—the white light of the Spirit of Jesus. They have caught the meaning of what it is to be a real Christian; in the light of that they are judging us. We could stand in the light of the civilization of other times and climes and feel on the whole that we have come off pretty well, but it is another thing to be judged in the light of his spirit and demand.

In speaking to an audience in India, I have often mentioned the incident of the church in South Africa with a sign on it, "Asiatics and Hottentots not allowed," and how Mahatma Gandhi could not get into the church because he was an Asian, and have ended up by saying that my own Master could not get into the church because he too was an Asian. I have noted the pained scorn that would go across the faces of the audience. But the audience was not especially conscious or disturbed that the low-caste people were excluded from their own temples, not by signs, but by the decree of religion and custom. In the one case they were judging themselves in the light of their own religion, but they were judging us in the light of the Spirit of Jesus. It is no answer, then, to say that they do the same things toward their own people—they are judging us by the religion we avow and by the Christ whom we profess to follow, and they have a right to do so. I am personally glad that they are doing it—cut as it may—for our salvation as well as theirs depends upon our being brought back to his mind and purpose.

A thoughtful Hindu said to me one day, "If you call one of us a *Christian* man, he is complimented, but if you call him a *Christian*, he is insulted." In that penetrating statement we get the epitome of the situation: the designation of Christian may mean that he is a member of the Christian community—Indian or European—it may not mean much; but to call him a *Christian* man is to pay the highest compliment that can be paid. They see that to be a Christian man is to catch the Spirit of Jesus.

A little Hindu girl caught the meaning of what a real Christian is when she gave this definition of a Christian: "One who is different from all others."

But many of the Christians are not Christian. A Hindu in the great city of ——— said to me, "If you can show me one real Christian in this city, I'll be a Christian." Overstated? Yes, but it carries its meaning.

A Hindu teacher said to me one day, "I want to become a Christian, but I do so in spite of the lives of the Europeans I have seen here. They seem to have two loathings—one is religion and the other is water." And he did not mean it for bathing, but for drinking purposes! This was said in a section of the East—the Straits Settlements—where nearly every European planter had his native concubine. His race prejudices do not extend as far as his lusts.

I was in a certain city where two Europeans had fought a duel, and both had been killed. The Hindus, out of the kindness of their hearts, buried them, and wishing to make an offering to the spirits of the dead, after thinking the matter over, thought they would love in death what they had loved in life, so came and offered as an offering on the tomb a cigar box and a whisky bottle.

But it is not merely the lives of some local Europeans that are the great hindrance, but the whole wide world has now become a whispering gallery, and India is listening in. I have broadcast my messages a number of times since I came home, and it was uncanny to feel that my conversational tones spoken into a tiny disk in an obscure corner were being listened to hundreds and thousands of miles away. That thing is happening in a broader sense. What we are doing in legislative halls and in the seemingly obscure incidents of racial attitudes is being broadcast to the rest of the world—and there is a loudspeaker at the other end.

Listen to the loudspeaker in this story giving its message: I sat in the midst of a group of earnest Nationalists in a Round Table Conference. I said: "My brothers, I have been talking to you these nights about Christ. I want you to tell me frankly and openly why you do not accept him. Do not spare me, for I am not the issue—tell me frankly." A Hindu arose and said, "You ask us to be Christians; may we ask you how Christian is your own civilization? Don't you have corruption at your central government at Washington?" (It was just after the revelations of the Teapot Dome scandal at Washington when oil began to flow!)

Another asked, "Don't you lynch black people in America?"

A third: "You have had Christianity in the West all these centuries, and though Jesus is the Prince of Peace you have not yet learned the way out of war. Don't you know any more about Christianity than that?"

These things were not said in spleen and hatred, but in anxiety and thoughtfulness. The loudspeaker was speaking on the other side of the world.

Here is another scene that has its meaning. I was in a section of India where, just before our coming, there had been near riots over the question of the baptism of a Hindu girl. Indignation meetings had been held and the city was in turmoil. We held our meetings with this background of unrest and resentment. We wondered if we would get any hearing at all. To our surprise there were great crowds and a most respectful and interested hearing. The last night a room at the rear was filled with earnest seekers after new life through Christ. But on the threshold of that invitation to give themselves to Christ was this incident: At question time a voice came out of the back of the crowd, "What do you think of the KKK?" This was about four years ago, when I had scarcely heard of the Ku Klux Klan myself. But here in a backwater of India, a place where I thought the least from the outside would penetrate, the loudspeaker was speaking and was embarrassing our witness and message. I know many persons in the Klan, and they are sincere and earnest, but since they are a religious organization and have the cross at the center of their gatherings, their racial attitudes are a decided embarrassment to us.

The local whisper intended to deal with a local American problem was resounding around the world and cutting across the message we were giving to India.

Nothing spoke louder to that whole Eastern world than the recent action of Congress in passing the ill-advised and un-Christian Immigration Law.[2] I wish America could see what she did in that bit of hasty legislation. Up to that time America held the moral leadership of the East. It was a moral asset to be an American. Japan was grateful for what we had done by our wonderful generosity after the 1923 Great Kanto Earthquake; China was more than friendly because of the Boxer indemnity incident and our traditional attitude of friendliness, and India was moved by the idealism of President Wilson and the realism of what we had actually done in bringing the Philippine Islands so quickly to practical self-government. In Persia we were loved and respected because of the help that disinterested Americans had given to assist Persia to her feet financially, as this incident shows: I was among the Syrian refugees in Baghdad. They had fled before the Kurds from Urumiyah, Persia. The watch that I currently wear was given to me by the

2. This is a reference to the Immigration Act of 1924, which effectively barred immigration from Asia, set quotas for other regions, and created the Border Patrol and visa requirements for entering the United States.

Syrians for what I was able to do for them in their time of trouble. But this was nothing compared to the gratitude another section of them felt when they fled for protection to the compound of the American Mission in Persia. As the Kurds came on, bent on blood, the missionary put out the American flag in front of the compound. The Kurdish leader did not know what flag it was. When told it was an American flag he advanced and was met by the missionary, who said, "This is an American flag, and in its name I ask for protection for the refugees here." The leader thought a moment, turned to his men and ordered them to retire. They were spared, protected by the flag. The refugees, overjoyed, kissed the flag that had delivered them. That is what the American flag stood for in the East at the close of the Great War and after. In one moment by this Immigration Law, we renounced the leadership that was in our hands.

We talk as if this were a problem for the Japanese, but India and China are put in the same position as Japan.

Do not misunderstand me. I am not advocating the flooding of America by immigrants. My own views are embodied in the resolution passed by the Federal Council of Churches of America and the last General Conference of the Methodist Episcopal Church:

"We urge a federal law raising the standards for admission into the United States, applying them to all nations alike, and granting the privilege of citizenship to all those thus admitted who duly qualify regardless of their race, color, or nationality."

This would mean that we could put the bars as high as we like, provided there is no racial discrimination and consequent insult.

If the present law were extended to apply to all nations alike, it would mean, according to the first provision of the law, namely, that 2 percent of the nationals of the 1890 census can be admitted, that 40 Japanese, 2,140 Chinese, and 42 East Indians would be admitted each year. But the second section of the law provides that "the annual quota of any nationality for the fiscal year beginning July 1, 1927, and for each fiscal year thereafter, shall be a number which bears the same ratio to 150,000 as the number of inhabitants in continental United States in 1920 having that national origin . . . bears to the number of inhabitants in continental United States in 1920." This would mean that after July 1, 1927, the number of Japanese admitted would be 159, Chinese 87, and East Indians 4, making a total of 250 people from Asia. This is nothing among a population of 114,000,000 and would never mean an economic or social problem. The fact is that the East is not keen to flood America. I was talking to an Indian official, the vice-president of the Legislative Assembly, and I said, "Suppose we should be able to get India put on a quota basis, it would mean that there would be actually less Indians admitted into America than before, for now about eight hundred or nine hundred are being admitted each year, largely according to the will of the American Consul in Calcutta; this would cut the number down to about four in all; would you not therefore feel that we had done India an injustice by having India put on a quota basis?" He replied: "We do not care how many of our people go to America. We do not want them to go, but we do not want them nationally insulted if they do go."

The fact of the matter is that many more than 250 are now being smuggled into America across the Mexican and Canadian borders and we have no redress. We can bring no pressure to bear upon the governments of these countries to stop this illicit smuggling, for the whole thing is too sore a point to raise with them, and they are in no mood to assist us in stopping it. The shortsightedness of Congress overreached itself and has left us in a worse condition regarding flooding than before. But I do not advocate the modification of the law because of the self-interest involved, nor because of its effects upon Christian missions, but because it is Christian to treat other nations as we ourselves would like to be treated.

It has been said that to repeal this law would be worth more than sending one hundred missionaries to the East. I should be inclined to doubt that estimate and to go further, and say, that in certain circles those missionaries who are there now will either mark time until it is repealed or win the people in spite of being Americans. I go back to the East with a heavy heart, knowing that I shall have to apologize for the attitude of the land of my birth to the land of my adoption. I shall meet it in every public meeting at question time, in nearly every personal conversation and in the changed attitude of sullen indifference. This legislation has broken our arms as we stretch them out in friendliness and good will toward the nations of the East, and yet it was from Asia that we got the one thing that is truly worthwhile in our civilization and the one thing that we look to to save us—Christ.

The Hindus have discovered that Jesus looked on man apart from race and birth and color; that he looked on man as man and believed in the sacredness of personality as such. They know that he was color blind and that the vision that he saw and that he aimed to transmit to others was that there is "one race, one color and one soul in humanity." In the white light of that conception, they are judging us. I have had this story concerning the origin of the white man quoted to me by an Indian: "God asked the man who is now white what he had done with his brother, and he turned white with fear." Read the book entitled *The Black Man's Burden* and you will come to the conclusion that there is enough truth in the above story to make it sting.[3]

---

3. This is most likely a reference to E. D. Morel, *The Black Man's Burden* (New York: B. W. Huebsch, 1920). In the introduction, Morel claims his book has a dual purpose: "It seeks to convey a clear notion of the atrocious wrongs which the white peoples have inflicted upon the black. It seeks to lay down the fundamental principles of a human and practical policy in the government of Africa by white men" (vii).

Mr. C. F. Andrews writes: "A Hindu gentleman of my acquaintance said to me, 'Do you not see what is happening? Mr. S——— is tearing down your work faster than you can build it up. Every time he calls us n—— it is a blow dealt to your religion, for you teach us that caste is sinful, while you Christians are building up a white caste of your own.'"

For the life of me I cannot see any essential difference between this white caste which we are building up and the Brahman caste of India, except that the former is based upon the color of the pigment of the skin with which one happens to be born, and the other is based upon the family into which birth brings one. They are both based upon the accidents of birth. If there is any real difference, it is in this, that the Brahman caste idea is according to his religion and has its sanction, and our white-caste idea is directly opposed to our faith and has its condemnation, and therefore of the two ours is the more hideous and reprehensible. Both should go.

A penetrating, but kindly old philosopher of India, Bara Dada, the brother of Dr. Rabindranath Tagore, pronounced this judgment: as we sat in the evening talking for long hours about these things he thoughtfully said, "Jesus is ideal and wonderful, but you Christians—you are not like him."

If we should be like him, if we should catch his spirit and outlook, what would happen? A Hindu lecturer on educational subjects was addressing an audience of educationalists in South India when he paused and said: "I see that a good many of you here are Christians. Now, this is not a religious lecture, but I would like to pause long enough to say that, if you Christians would live like Jesus Christ, India would be at your feet tomorrow." He said nothing less than the very truth.

Another Hindu put the matter just as strongly but in different words. He was a Hindu head judge of a native state and was the chairman of my meeting. At the close of the address, he spoke to the audience in these words: "You have heard tonight what it means to be a Christian. If to be like Christ is what it means, I hope you will all be Christians in your lives." Then turning to us who were Christians he said: "I have one word to speak to you: If you Christians had lived more like Jesus Christ, this process of conversion would have gone on much more rapidly." It was sincerely and truly said.

This judgment of the West by the East in the light of the person of Jesus is powerfully expressed in the lines which a Bengali poet wrote on Christmas Day and sent to my friend, Mr. C. F. Andrews:

> Great-souled Christ, on this the blessed day of your birth, we who are not Christians bow before you. We love and worship you, we non-Christians, for with Asia you are bound with the ties of blood.
>
> We, the puny people of a great country, are nailed to the cross of servitude. We look mutely up to you, hurt, and wounded at every turn of our torture—the foreign ruler over us the crown of thorns; our own social caste system the bed of spikes on which we lie.
>
> The world stands aghast at the earth hunger of Europe. Imperialism in the arms of Mammon dances with unholy glee. The three witches—War Lust, Power Lust, Profit Lust—revel on the barren hearths of Europe holding their orgies.
>
> "There is no room for thee there in Europe. Come, Lord Christ, come away! Take your stand in Asia—the land of Buddha, Kabir, and Nanak. At the sight of you our sorrow-laden hearts will be lightened. O Teacher of love, come down into our hearts and teach us to feel the sufferings of others, to serve the leper and the pariah with an all-embracing love.

This poetic appeal loses none of its power of judgment and appeal even if we could have wished that he had said that instead of Christ coming away he had asked that he would enter more deeply into the life of the West. Come, Lord Christ, come away? Nay, Lord Christ, do not go away! For we too have sorrow-laden hearts; and if the East is crucified on a cross of servitude, we are being crucified on a cross of materialism. We both need thee—desperately.

This judgment of the East is a call calling us back to our own Master and Lord. As such we welcome it. It shocks us from our smug complacency. It is the earthquake that does not destroy us but looses our chains. It is the angel that smites us and says, "Arise." This searching criticism of the East is a Godsend to keep us from falling asleep after taking an overdose of the opiate of material prosperity. It is God's own voice to us. It is stabbing us awake.

This story tells what I mean. An Indian Christian doctor came to see me one morning in a far-off hill station. He said he was deeply troubled in mind. He unfolded this story: "I was a ship's doctor. In Hong Kong I met a Parsee with whom I became friendly. One day he turned to me and said, 'Are you living the Christian life?' 'It is impossible,' I answered. 'Difficult but not impossible,' he replied, 'for His living Presence gives you power.' I found that though he was a Parsee he was more of a Christian than I was. When my boat sailed back to India, my Parsee friend was on the dock to see me off. As the ship pulled off from the dock, he put his hands to his mouth and shouted to me across the widening gulf, 'Remember, seek ye first the kingdom of God and his righteousness, and all these things shall be added unto you.' The sight of that Parsee and the sound of his voice calling to me that phrase 'Seek first the Kingdom' have haunted me. I haven't been seeking the Kingdom first. I have come to you to pray with me." There we knelt, and that fine doctor made the surrender and arose, adjusted to the will of Christ—and happy. The Kingdom was to be first! But the anomaly: a Parsee had led him to it!

Across the widening gulf between East and West I see the awakened East, realizing how deeply endangered we are by materialism and racism and knowing that only as we are saved can we save them, putting its hands to its lips and calling to us of the West, "Seek first the kingdom of God." May it haunt and woo us to repentance and to Christ as it did my Indian brother! Only thus can we turn back and share and save.

The situation is summed up in the words of a far-seeing Christian thinker and statesman: "We recognize that conditions in the West demand an indubitable and pervasive humility on the part of Christians, and that a deep sense of national and racial repentance should accompany any further missionary work that we may do."

These brave words of the Christian thinker agree with the penetrating but kindly counsel of India's great soul, Mahatma Gandhi. In conversation with him one day I said, "Mahatma Gandhi, I am very anxious to see Christianity naturalized in India, so that it shall be no longer a foreign thing identified with a foreign people and a foreign government, but a part of the national life of India and contributing its power to India's uplift and redemption. What would you suggest that we do to make that possible?" He very gravely and thoughtfully replied: "I would suggest, first, that all of you Christians, missionaries and all, must begin to live more like Jesus Christ." He needn't have said anything more—that was quite enough. I knew that looking through his eyes were the three hundred million of India and speaking through his voice were the voiceless millions of the East saying to me, a representative of the West, and through me to that very West itself, "If you will come to us in the spirit of your Master, we cannot resist you." Never was there a greater challenge to the West than that, and never was it more sincerely given. "Second," he said, "I would suggest that you must practice your religion without adulterating or toning it down." This is just as remarkable as the first.

The greatest living non-Christian asks us not to adulterate it or tone it down, not to meet them with an emasculated gospel, but to take it in its rugged simplicity and high demand. But what are we doing? As someone has suggested, we are inoculating the world with a mild form of Christianity, so that it is now practically immune against the real thing. Vast areas of the Christian world are inoculated with a mild form of Christianity, and the real thing seems strange and impossible. As one puts it, "Our churches are made up of people who would be equally shocked to see Christianity doubted or put into practice." I am not anxious to see India take a mild form—I want her to take the real thing. "Third, I would suggest that you must put your emphasis upon love, for love is the center and soul of Christianity." He did not mean love as a sentiment, but love as a working force, the one real power in a moral universe, and he wanted it applied between individuals and groups and races and nations, the one cement and salvation of the world. With a soul so sensitive to the meaning of love, no wonder there were tears in his eyes when I read him at that point the thirteenth chapter of First Corinthians. "Fourth, I would suggest that you study the non-Christian religions and culture more sympathetically in order to find the good that is in them, so that you might have a more sympathetic approach to the people." Quite right. We should be grateful for any truth found anywhere, knowing that it is a finger post that points to Jesus, who is the Truth.

When I mentioned these four things to the Chief Justice of the High Court in North India, the noble, sympathetic, Christian Britisher exclaimed: "He could not have put his finger on four more important things. It took spiritual genius and insight to do that."

When I asked another nationalist leader the same question as to what we must do to naturalize Christianity, he replied, "You must have more men like ——— and ———," naming two men among the missionaries who were devoted lovers of Christ and of India.

Here, then, is the epitome of the whole thing: From every side they say we must be Christian, but Christian in a bigger, broader way than we have hitherto been.

* * *

One word of caution: Some who have little love for endeavors of uplift for those outside their own racial group may seize on the above chapter as a justification for withdrawing everything from others and concentrating it upon themselves, forgetting that this is a disastrous fallacy, for the moment we cease to share with others where there is seemingly no return and recompense to ourselves, that moment we cease to be Christian. We cannot be Christian and concentrate ourselves on ourselves. America can never be Christian apart from its world task.

> "Oh, East is East and West is West,
> And never the twain shall meet."[4]
> So spake a son of man—and erred!
>
> Oh, man is man and man with man shall meet,
> So taught the Son of man, and at his feet,
> Bade us there learn the worth of *human* worth;
> To see the man apart from race and birth.
>
> To find in Aryan pale and Aryan brown,
> In Mongol and in sun-blacked African;
> The oneness of humanity—the same
> God-touched, aspiring, worthful soul of man.

* * *

> Boast not, Oh Aryan pale, o'er Aryan brown,
> Of greatness not in thee—'tis in the gift!

4. This quotation is from the opening lines of Rudyard Kipling's "The Ballad of East and West" (1889). The rest of the poem was written by Jones.

For, once, a nail-pierced Hand of Asia touched
 Thy life and grants thee now his gracious lift.

Beware, lest in the roll of judging years,
 That Hand, withdrawn from thee through pride of race,
May touch to power those races now despised,
 And grant to them thy forfeit—power and place.

The Master bids thee lose thy petty self
 In service, and thy help to brothers give;
And thou shalt truly find thyself again,
 'Twill be thy gain, and others too shall live.

Thus freed from tribal mind and attitude,
 Thy Christianed soul, with self-renounced, shall find
A larger, richer self of brotherhood;
 Since, with the Christ, it has the Kingdom mind.

A Kingdom where there is no East nor West;
 There are no walls dividing clan from clan;
But brotherhood as wide as humankind,
 And with a King who is the "Son of man."

* * *

Oh, man is man, and man with man shall meet,
So speaks the Son of man. O Master! shamed,
But learning, sit we here—here at thy feet.

CHAPTER VII

THE QUESTION HOUR

WHILE at one of the university centers of America, it was announced that I would answer questions at the close if the audience desired. Among those who stayed were many students, American and foreign, and among them some Hindus from India. These Hindu students put me through a grilling for several hours. At the close I remarked to someone: "This is the first time I have really felt at home in America. I feel as though I have been in India tonight." After almost every meeting in India we allow the non-Christians to ask questions—and grilled we are!

When I began to throw open my meetings in India for questions, I knew I was inviting disaster, for the Hindu mind is quite as good as ours, and it loves argument. Besides the possibility of having everything you have said in your address upset by questions, I was quite conscious of another danger. Christianity cannot be understood except in a quiet mood of moral and spiritual receptivity and insight. Questions often change the quiet atmosphere to one of belligerency. Nevertheless, there was so much misunderstanding, so much rejecting of a caricature of Christianity, that I felt we should face everything fairly and dodge no issue.

I would not have dared to do it had I not been given in the very beginning of this work a verse that has seemed my very own: "And when they shall deliver you up before kings and governors for my name's sake for a testimony unto them, be not anxious what ye shall speak, for it shall be given you in that hour what ye shall speak, for it is not ye that speak, but the spirit of your Father which speaketh in you" (Matthew 10:18-20). That assurance was sufficient for me. I believed it. I could do nothing less.

The question hour becomes tense at times, but we have tried to make it a point never to let it degenerate into a mere quibble, or to allow it to stir bad blood. To lose one's temper would be to lose one's case, for we are not there to win arguments, but to win men. I cannot remember when ill feeling has been left after any single meeting. We have tried to demonstrate incidentally that one can discuss these thorny questions with quiet good humor.

There is an amazing range of questions from those of a confused, but spiritually earnest, questioner, to the questions of the quibbler who desires to show off his smartness. To let you see what questions India is asking, I give a few samples taken almost at random from many hundreds sent up:

Ques.—Is Christianity a universal religion? If so, why are there sectional feelings going on? Catholics hate Protestants, the Greek Church contradicts both.

Ques.—Why did God make a world where he ought to have known evil would come, where brutes who trade on hunger, who convert into coin the patience of the poor, the sweat of slaves, would exist? Where rascally sycophants would have power and righteous men rot in jails; where, in short, Christ would be crucified? Who is responsible for such a world?

Ques.—Do you sincerely believe that there are many fine Christians having the true democratic spirit of Christ? How do you account for the feeling of racial superiority which the Westerners have? What Christian spirit is that which makes Australians, the Canadians, and the people of America prevent Indians from coming into their country and enjoying equal privileges with them?

Ques.—Does not the present war—a war among the followers of Christ—prove that there is something wrong with the teachings of Christ?

Ques.—Suppose that from four corners in a square, four men desire to get to the center. They will go in different directions, but they will get to the center. There are different religions, but they all lead to the center: God. But the ways are not the same. Why do you say there is only one way? There are many ways. You cannot prescribe the same drug for every disease.

Ques.—In your lecture last evening you took it for granted that all the stories in the gospel are true. Is it not possible that the writers, who were not men of culture, either distorted the facts or exaggerated them? Could it not be that their enthusiasm misled them into wrong judgments and that they wrote out even false rumors among the ignorant masses?

Ques.—I will pay Christianity the compliment of thinking that if the world were ruled by strict Christian tenets, it would be a semi-paradise. But the grim fact of our experience is that it is the Christian that has by iniquitous means come by the major portion of this planet, which he keeps under his iron rod. So, is it not more proper that the missionaries, with their gifts of head and heart, endeavored to moralize their own coreligionists instead of pursuing the wild-goose chase of conversion, for, after all, numbers are absolutely irrelevant to the greatness of a faith?

Ques.—How is it that divorces are a part of Christianity in the West?

Ques.—Is King George a real Christian? Then, pointing to a prominent Indian Christian in front, he asked, "Is Mr. J —— here a real Christian?"

Ques.—Don't you think we could put Islam and Christianity together? Jesus lived a very high, a very lofty, a very ideal, a very sinless life, and he did not marry. Mohammed did marry, so I suggest that when we put these two religions together, we make Jesus the theory or ideal of the religion and Mohammed the practice.

Ques.—We are two young men who after hearing your addresses desire to become Christians. But as you seem to be a holy man, we would like to test your powers; we are not going to sign this letter—can you tell us who we are?

Ques.—Why do Christians wear neckties? Is it the sign of the Cross or is it a custom?

Ques.—How is it that women in Christianity are in the lowest degradation, they are considered an object of scorn, they have no rights of any kind, while in Islam when Mohammed said, "What is due from her is due to her," he raised her at one bound to an equality with man? Is this no improvement on Christianity? (Sent in by a Muslim.)

Ques.—If salvation of human beings lies only through faith in Jesus, what is to happen to those who cannot sincerely believe in the Christian gospel?

Ques.—What is to happen to the souls of those who have never had the opportunity of hearing the gospel of Christ?

Ques.—If I suffer for my misdeeds, and if it is right before God and man that I should suffer, why should a man in his ignorance come and help me in the name of love? Is he not unconsciously weakening my cause, and thwarting God's plan and Nature's law? Is not the social servant an indiscreet almsgiver?

Ques.—It is again said that after man fell even then God did not forsake him, but devised a plan by which he might be restored to a great happiness that he lost. And what forsooth is this "plan"? Why, he sent his Son to die for them, and this also after having allowed thousands of years to pass by and millions of people hopelessly to perish and to go to that place of torment called "hell," which he had prepared for them. Now, is this not an old woman's tale such as the nurses frighten the babes withal?

Ques.—Why does a Hindu accept Christ, but reject Christianity?

Ques.—Can moral life, even if it is touched with emotion, satisfy the human soul which is yearning for the imperishable and eternal union with the Eternal Spirit transcending all limitations of space and relativity?

Ques.—Is the world safe for Christ? If Christ were to come today among the Christian nations of the earth, do you think he would not be crucified?

Ques.—Can one be a Christian without baptism?

Ques.—Do you think that to be a follower of Christ fully and truly one should accept Christian dogma also? Would you agree with the Frenchman who defined dogma as the living faith of the dead and the dead faith of the living?

Ques.—May it be pointed out in all humility and reverence that it is necessary to preach Christ instead of Christianity to India?

Ques.—Is the idea of redemption peculiar to Christianity and foreign to other religions? Do you not think that the idea of God as Friend and Companion is the insistent note of the non-monistic school of Indian thought such as Vaishnavism?

Ques.—If Christianity is fitted to become a universal religion, what new and exclusive truths has it to teach over and above what other great religions like Hinduism or Buddhism have taught?

Ques.—If a religion should appeal to men of different natures and temperaments in order to claim universal acceptance, then has not Hinduism, which shows three paths, namely, Gnana, Karma, and Bhakti, better claim to it, than Christianity, which indicates only the paths of love and Bhakti?

Ques.—Is not Hinduism, which teaches belief in a personal as well as impersonal God, more satisfying to less developed as well as more developed souls alike than Christianity, which teaches only the former?

Ques.—As materialism, luxury, and intemperance have been known to follow in the wake of Christianity, how can it appeal to the Hindus, whose outlook on life and its problems is preeminently spiritual?

Ques.—As Christianity has no system of philosophy behind it, but is only a God of ethical conduct, how is it suited to satisfy the philosophically minded Hindu race?

Ques.—If Jesus is only a God-man, as you said yesterday, what better claim has he than other equally great God-men like Buddha or Rama, Krishna, Paramahamsa, to become a universal teacher?

Ques.—What tests shall I perform, if any, to understand the saving power of Christ?

My most difficult moments are not with the written questions, but in those meetings where oral questions are shot at one. I have been cross-examined by as many as thirty lawyers at one time trying for hours to beat down the evidence. But my verse has been true. I cannot remember a single situation in nine years where it has failed me. There have been some very close calls! For instance, one night a man arose and asked, "Can you put your finger on a verse where Jesus calls himself the Son of God? Not where his disciples or someone else called him that, but where he himself did." A sinking feeling went over me. I had a rather hazy notion about where there was such a passage, but I couldn't remember just where it was, and he wanted me to put my finger on it! I turned to my New Testament with a prayer to find that verse. As I opened it the first verse my eyes fell upon was an entirely different one from the one I was looking for, the one where Jesus met the man whom he had healed and asked him if he believed on the Son of God. The man replied, "Who is he, Lord, that I might believe on him?" Jesus replied, "Thou hast both seen him, and he it is that speaketh unto thee." I read it off as if I had known about it all the time! They never knew the quiet little miracle that God had performed to fulfill his promise that it should be given in that hour what one should speak! But I knew and thanked him.

I have found a good many nervous Christians since coming home who are afraid that this whole thing of Christianity might fall to pieces if someone should get too critical or if science should get too scientific. Many of the saints are now painfully nervous. They remind me of a lady missionary with whom I walked home one night after a very tense meeting in a Hindu theater. She said, "Mr. Jones, I am physically exhausted from that meeting tonight." When I asked her the reason she said, "Well, I didn't know what they were going to ask you next, and I didn't know what you were going to answer, so I've been sitting up there in the gallery holding on to the bench with all my might for two hours, and I'm physically exhausted!" There are many like our sister who are metaphorically holding to their seats with all their might lest Christianity fall to pieces under criticism!

I have a great deal of sympathy with them, for I felt myself in the same position for a long time after I went to India. The whole atmosphere was acid with criticism. I could feel the acid eat into my very soul every time I picked up a non-Christian paper. Then there came the time when I inwardly let go. I became willing to turn Jesus over to the facts of the universe. I began to see that there was only one refuge in life and that was in reality, in the facts. If Jesus couldn't stand the shock of the criticism of the facts discovered anywhere, if he wasn't reality, the sooner I found it out the better. My willingness to surrender Christ to the facts was almost as great an epoch in my life as my willingness to surrender to him. In the moment of letting go I could almost feel myself inwardly turning pale. What would happen? Would the beautiful dream fade? To my happy amazement I found that he not only stood, but that he shone as never before. I saw that he was not a hothouse plant that would wither under the touch of criticism, but he was rooted in reality, was the very living expression of our moral and spiritual universe—he was reality itself.

I have, therefore, taken my faith and have put it out before the non-Christian world for these seventeen years and have said, "There it is, my brothers, break it if you can." And the more they have smitten upon it the more it has shone. Christ came out of the storms and will weather them. The only way to kill Christianity is to take it out of life and protect it. The way to make it shine and show its genius is to put it down in life and let it speak directly to life itself. Jesus is his own witness. The Hindus have formed societies called *Dharm Raksha Sabhas*—Societies for the Protection of Religion. Jesus does not need to be protected. He needs to be presented. He protects himself.

I could therefore reply to my sister mentioned above that in that stormy meeting I had been having the time of my life, that I wanted them to go into the matter, for if they would only go deep enough, they would stand face to face with Jesus. For he did not come to bring a way of life—he came to be Life itself, and if they go deep enough into life, they would find themselves facing Jesus, who is Life itself. He did not come to bring a set of truths to set alongside of other truths, as some have superficially imagined, he came to be Truth; and if one goes far enough with truth, it will lead him by the hand till he faces him who is Truth itself. Dean Inge rightly says, "Jesus did not come to bring a religion but to be Religion," and if we are seriously religious, we will have to be according to his mind and spirit or else fail to be religious. In the language of Matthew Arnold, "Jesus is an Ultimate."

Start in at the thing that you know is worthwhile and follow it back to its final form and see where it lands you. For instance, love is a worthwhile thing in life. We ought to love. Then trace love back to its ultimate kind and you will not be far from Him who loved as never man loved. If purity is a good thing, then start with it and go on back and see what kind of ultimate purity it brings you to, and you will find yourself looking into the eyes of Him who was "the Purest among the mighty, and the Mightiest among the pure." If self-sacrifice is life's most noble quality, then run it back to its finest type and you will find yourself gazing upon a cross.

I am therefore not afraid of the question hour, for I believe that Jesus underlies our moral and spiritual universe deeper than the force of gravity underlies our material universe. And although I know I cannot answer many things—for the case is bigger than the pleader—I believe that some way, somehow, some time, human minds, groping like the tendril of the vine that reaches out for the wall and finally touching it fastens itself upon its solid reality, will ultimately fasten upon Jesus as that Reality.

But more difficult to meet than the question hour is when they test us not with questions but by whether we have truly caught the Christ spirit. The big question that India silently and relentlessly asks is not, How keen a mind has he? But, Has he the mind of Christ?

This was brought vividly home to me one day when two Hindu youths, dressed very plainly and in bare feet, came to talk with me. I had had many interviews that day, but none of them did I enjoy like the hour I had with these young men. They were so eager and alert and responsive. The next day they came again, this time to make an explanation. They told me who they were—sons of the wealthiest and most prominent people in the city. They had purposely come the day before barefoot and with very poor clothes on to test me, to see whether I really meant it when I had said the preceding night that Jesus looked on people as such, apart from race and birth and color and possessions, and whether I would practice it in my attitude toward them dressed in poor clothes! They said that they had previously thought of becoming Christians and determined to make this a test as to whether they would or not. It was all done so naïvely and simply that one could not but feel it was genuine, especially when they said they were now ready to become Christians.

This event did not elate me, it sobered me, for the serious thought kept haunting me, how easy it would have been to have said the careless word and to have assumed a patronizing attitude—both of which I had often done—when so much hung upon the slightest act or attitude!

India is asking questions; those that she asks with her lips are serious and searching, but of far more vital concern are the silent weighings and inward judgments of us by which India comes to her conclusions about Christ.

The High Priest asked Jesus "of his disciples and of his teaching." The non-Chistian world is asking those same two things and always in that order. "What life have you?" "What light have you?"

> I took my lamp and went and sat
> Where men of another creed and custom
> Dwelt together in bonds of common search.

I pressed my lamp close to my bosom,
Lest adverse winds of thought and criticism,
And the damp of unsympathy should snuff it out.
And many a trembling prayer hung upon my lips.

But I determined that I would love—just love.
I loved and listened and learned, and now and then
Threw in a thought or word or observation.
I heard their gentle speech, saw their mild ways;
Felt the Hand of Peace rest gently on my soul.
Here was not the tearing of the flesh,
Nor the fierce agony of the spirit, in its quest for God.

They gently searched and, through the crevices of their thought,
The light of our Father's Face streamed in.
They caught the footfalls of the Mighty Spirit,
As he moved each moment through palpitating Nature.
And I heard them tune their heartstrings to catch the music
Of God, as he hummed and sang through things.

But when, in sympathetic talk and mutual quest,
I asked the learned pundit whether he had found
A "jiwan mukta," one who knew deliverance, here and now;
He sadly shook his head and said, "I have not seen."
In his voice spoke an aching world: "I have not seen."
Then there stole within my heart a quiet joy;
For I saw, amid the search of peoples and races,
One standing, who, with Chalice in hand, offered here and now
To thirsty souls a crystal draught of life eternal,
Which, if a man drink, he shall never thirst again.

Had I not drunk? Had he not put the Chalice
To my parched lips and, with thirst assuaged,
Had not my happy soul gone singing down the years?
A child had thus revealed to him, through prayer and
Surrender of the mind and will, that for which

The wise and prudent had vainly searched
And caught but glimpses; while I, unworthy,
Stood face to Face.

As I pondered thus, I glanced, with trembling, at my lamp—
And lo, it burned up brighter than before!

CHAPTER VIII

Jesus Through Experience

RELIGION is the life of God in the soul issuing in the kingdom of God on earth. But first of all, it is the life of God in the soul. Religion means realization. If not, then religion soon means ritual, and that means death.

The early disciples had little ritual but a mighty realization. They went out not remembering Christ but realizing him. They did not merely call him back into memory, they communed with him in the deeps. He was not a mere fair and beautiful story to remember with gratitude—he was a living, redemptive, actual Presence then and there. They went out with the joyous and grateful cry, "Christ lives in me!" The Jesus of history had become the Christ of experience. They were almost irresistible, for they brought certainty into that uncertain world. Pliny the Elder had said, "There is nothing certain save the absence of certainty," and Plato longed for "some sure word from God" that would be a raft to carry him across the uncertain seas of human existence. The apostles brought certainty.

Someone has suggested that the early Christians conquered that pagan world because they out-thought, they outlived and they out-died the pagans. But that was not enough: they out-experienced them. Without that, it would have lacked the vital glow. If the word of Christ becomes paramount in India, it will be because those who follow him out-experience those who do not follow him. When Elijah stood upon Mount Carmel, he made this the test: "The God that answers by fire, let him be God" (1 Kings 18:24). The test of the surviving God is now different. We say, "The God that answers by producing radiant healed men, let him be God." It is just that certain note that needs to be struck in India. Not the note of aggressive dogmatism, but the persuasive note of Christian experience.

If, as someone suggests, all great literature is autobiography, then all great appeals to the non-Christian world must be a witness. Henry Drummond would never preach anything that had not first gone through his own experience, and Drummond therefore spoke with power.

Doctor J. N. Farquhar said to me regarding this matter: "There are two things that are almost irresistible to the Indian mind just now—Christ and Christian experience." I agreed most heartily, for it was the thing I had been driven to: Christ must be interpreted through Christian experience.

But the Hindu has this reservation: he does not feel that a religious experience should be shouted from the housetops, he feels that to do this would be indelicate and would take away its bloom and beauty. Results should be whispered to one's neighbors. Doctor Tagore told me of the man whom he had found who had come into a great spiritual experience. He asked him if he was not going to tell it to the world? "No," he said; "if it is real, they will come to me." When I told the head pundit of an ashram that I had found one Hindu who said he was a jiwan mukta—one who had found living salvation—he replied, "He was not one if he said he was one." I can share the hesitancy of the Hindu when he feels the indelicacy of speaking about it.

But the genius and glory of Christian experience is that we have not earned it—it is a gift, absolutely undeserved and unmerited. When one accepts it, he loses all thought of the part he has had in it, and rapturously thinks of the Giver. It is not boasting, it is testimony. It is sharing with others what has been shared with us. We are to be witnesses on behalf of Another.

The Christ of the Indian Road pauses as he passes through the throngs and says, "Who touched me?" Knowing what the healing has meant to us, we can only acknowledge that our trembling touch upon him has meant life to us.

This lesson of being a witness was burned into my very being by a tragic beginning of my Christian ministry. When I was called to the ministry, I had a vague notion that I was to be God's lawyer—I was to argue his case for him and put it up brilliantly. When I told my pastor of my call he surprised and thoroughly frightened me by asking me to preach my first sermon on a certain Sunday night. I prepared very thoroughly, for I was anxious to make a good impression and argue his case acceptably. There was a large crowd there full of expectancy, for they wished the young man well. I began on rather a high key. I had not gone a half dozen sentences when I used a word I had never used before (nor have I used it since!)—"indifferentism." When I used that word, I saw a college girl in the audience put down her head and smile. It so upset me that when I came back to the thread of my discourse it was gone—absolutely. I do not know how long I stood there rubbing my hands hoping that something would come back. It seemed an age. Finally, I blurted out, "Friends, I am very sorry, but I have forgotten my sermon!" I started down the steps leading from the pulpit in shame and confusion. This was the beginning of my ministry, I thought—a tragic failure. As I was about to leave the pulpit a Voice seemed to say to me, "Haven't I done anything for you?"

"Yes," I replied, "You have done everything for me."

"Well," answered the Voice, "couldn't you tell that?"

"Yes, I suppose I could," I eagerly replied. So instead of going to my seat I came around in front of the pulpit below (I felt very lowly by this time and was persuaded I did not belong up there!) and said: "Friends, I see I cannot preach, but I love Jesus Christ. You know what my life was in this community—that of a wild, reckless young man—and you know what it now is. You know he has made life new for me, and though I cannot preach I am determined to love and serve him." At the close a lad came up and said, "Stanley, I wish I could find what you have found." He did find it then and there. He is a member of that church now—a fine Christian man. No one congratulated me on that sermon that night, but after the sting of it had passed away, I have been congratulating myself ever since. The Lord let me down with a terrible thump, but I got the lesson never to be forgotten: In my ministry I was to be, not God's lawyer, but his witness. That would mean that there would have to be living communion with Christ so that there would always be something to pass on. Since that day I have tried to witness before high and low what Christ has been to an unworthy life.

India wants to know: What have you found? The students at a Hindu college asked me to come and to speak to them at the college and they suggested the topic: "Tell your own personal religious experience." Always, on the last night of every series, I tell my personal experience. They forget many, if not most, of my arguments, but they bring up this matter of experience again and again. Experience grips us.

While I was telling of my conversion in ——— I noticed a Hindu college professor nodding his head with evident delight. At the close he came up eagerly, gripped my hand and said: "Oh, that is it. It is the new birth we need." The next day he showed me a schoolbook he had written for use in government colleges. It was annotations on Macaulay's *History of England*. Macaulay has given the Puritans a thrust, saying that during the Puritan reign the students, instead of studying the classics, were interrogated as to how and when and in what circumstances they received the new birth. This non-Christian professor took up Macaulay in the matter and in his comments said, "The pity is that Macaulay did not understand the new birth." Then he quoted the whole of the Nicodemus episode and finished up by saying, "Alas, the Nicodemuses today do not understand how these things can be." Here was a non-Christian professor criticizing a Christian historian for his lack of appreciation of the new birth! To lead a man like that professor, we must have something real and vital.

One day I was in the train with a Hindu lawyer, and we discussed, almost argued, for about three hours concerning Hindu and Christian philosophy and teaching. I saw we were getting nowhere, so I turned to him and said, "Would you mind my telling you what Christ has done for me?"

He eagerly replied, "No, I would like to hear."

When I got through telling of my conversion and the subsequent years there were tears in his eyes, and he said: "Mr. Jones, you have attained. You have reached the last stage of your rebirths. You will never be reborn into this world."

"That is probably true," I replied, "for one does not have to go through a weary round of rebirths as you expect to, for here is the new birth open to you—a straight, shortcut to the Father." There was deep earnestness again when he said, "I wish I had that." In his voice spoke the voice of India—it is deliverance from rebirths that India craves.

A Hindu student wrote to me, "After attending your addresses I want to be a follower of Christ, for I now see that my religion is a somewhat roundabout method of obtaining the kingdom of God." Somewhat roundabout! Yes, eight million rebirths, maybe. No wonder they shrink from such a prospect—from life itself. It is a joy to offer the new birth as the way out.

Here is a letter to me from a Jain student which speaks its own message of longing for spiritual freedom:

> I have deep faith in my own religion. I believe it to be entirely true, but I need not be ashamed to tell that it exacts unflinching duty and knows no grace. Philosophically it is all right. You may believe, according to it, that the Power behind things is supremely just and indifferent, but we err we know not why, we are led on as it were on the waves of sin and mistakes. There are powers too great for our frail being, and I wish then that there were a God who would be kind to me, who would feel my weaknesses and who would extricate me from the meshes of sin and temptation.

Can we come to a young man like that with an argument, a doctrine, a superior Book? Unless we can gently and quietly but with a radiant positiveness share with that young man our own deliverance and victory, we had better not come. Has Christ any answer to a letter like that? Here is the crux of the whole thing—Has he, or has he not? Some of us, knowing that we were there, in that very condition, believe that he has.

Let me pause here just long enough to say that here is where a good deal of present-day presentation is weak. That young man needs something more than Jesus as Example and Teacher. What he needed was not a Sage, but a Savior, not a moral Example but a moral Extractor, not a Redirector but a Regenerator, not truths but Life.

In a class of Hindu and Muslim students at the Ashram at ——— one of the students spoke up suddenly and said, "Sir, would you mind telling us what has made your life what it is?" It rather shocked me for a moment. It was a bolt out of the blue, as there was nothing that had led up to this. It was so absolutely spontaneous and real that I could but stop and quietly and prayerfully tell them how Christ had taken an unworthy broken life, and had made it whole again, and had sent my happy soul singing its way down these twenty years. When I had finished, one of them spoke up and said: "Now, sir, we are happy. That is what we wanted to hear." After the class some of them came with me to my room and we sat and talked for hours about it. In the afternoon some of the young ladies wanted an appointment. When I asked them what they wanted to talk about, one of them answered and said: "We were deeply impressed by what you said about your own personal experience this morning. Do you mind telling us something more about it?" And there we sat a long time upon the floor with the touch of the living Christ upon us all. Our hearts burned within us as we talked with him and about him, by the way.

The Indian people are as sensitive to spiritual things as the electric needle is to the pull of the pole. In one place a Hindu committee asked not to have questions at the close of the meeting, "for," they said, "it disturbs the beautiful spiritual atmosphere of the meetings." I saw a Hindu professor go out at the close of the address one night when the questions began. When the questions were through and I suggested that we might close the meeting with prayer, I saw him come in from the veranda. At the close of the prayer he came up and thanked me and said: "I went out after your address and stood on the veranda until the questions were over, for in your address you had lifted us to God and I did not want that feeling I had in my heart dissipated or disturbed by the questions, so I waited outside for the prayer, since in the prayer you made us again realize his presence." One feels awed in the presence of such beautiful spiritual sensitiveness as that.

A Hindu came up one night after the prayer and said, "That was very fine, but why don't you begin the meetings with prayer?" I assented and said I would do so the next night. But in the anxiety to get in the thick of the battle, I went into the address without public prayer. Of course, one could not get into such a tense situation where every word and idea is being challenged without preceding it with an hour or more of prayer, but I did not pray publicly. While I was speaking I saw a note coming up; the chairman handed it over to me. It read, "Sir, you forgot to begin your meeting with prayer, as you had promised." I stopped my address, acknowledged my fault, prayed, and went on. But I never forgot the undertone of spiritual yearning which that little incident revealed.

After I had had a long talk with a Hindu one day as he was about to go, I suggested that if he liked, we might pray together. "Yes," he said, "I will be glad to do so, but on one condition, and that is, that you do not pray for things but only for God."

"All right, my brother," I replied, "we will not pray for things but only for God," and we did! Could one face that hour without a deep sense of need for reality and a joyous sense of God? It is not a question as to whether we would or would not interpret Christ through experience—we must. Or else there is no interpretation that is adequate or touches the depths of the situation. We cannot merely talk about Christ to India—we must bring him. He must be a living vital reality—closer than breathing and nearer than hands and feet. We must be "God-bearers."

This God-consciousness should be full and overflowing. A Hindu lawyer recognized this and said to me one day, "What you Christians and the church need today is a new Pentecost." I knew what he meant—we need Christianity as a well of water within us springing up into everlasting life. Principal L. P. Jacks pleads that we get back "the lost radiance of the Christian religion."[1] Strange to hear a Hindu and a Unitarian both pleading for a new fullness of life akin to Pentecost! Even so, Pentecost is normal Christianity. But the church is largely subnormal and anemic. Because a few have gone up into fever and have done strange things in the name of this great

1. L. P. Jacks, *The Lost Radiance of the Christian Religion* (New York: George H. Doran, 1924).

Sanifying and Sanctifying of the human spirit by the inflooding of the Spirit of the living Christ, there is no reason why all the rest of us should be frightened away into an anemic Christianity. This Christ of the Indian Road is saying, "Receive ye the Holy Ghost," as well as, "Thy sins are forgiven thee."

A friend of mine was preaching in the bazaar in North India when a Hindu came up to him and said, "I want to ask a question, not through criticism but for information. I have been reading the New Testament and am especially struck with the Acts of the Apostles. These men seemed to have had a wonderful power and fullness of spiritual life. Sir, have you found what they had?" My friend was speechless. Though he was a graduate of a university and was a missionary, he knew in the inmost depths of being that he did not have what the early disciples seemed to have found. He went home, fell on his knees, yielded himself fully to Christ, and found! His life became one of the richest and most beautiful I have ever been privileged to see. When he died a few years ago, an Indian minister said, "It is a good thing that ——— did not die in India, for we would have committed the sin of worshipping his grave."

India is reading the Bible and wants to know whether our Christianity is like that. An Indian boy, whose zeal and love were better than his English, wrote to me about a great awakening they were having: "We are having a great re-bible here." Not a bad mistake! We need to be rebibled—especially at the place of the Acts of the Apostles.

It was said of those early apostles that they "testified and preached." Their preaching was throbbing with testimony. Since it came from the heart, it reached the heart. The last night of a series of meetings in South India I spoke on "Christ and Certainty." On the inspiration of the moment before closing the meeting I said, "Now there are quite a number of Christians here. I would like you to tell before your non-Christian friends in a very few words what you have found—what has Christ done for you?" First of all, there stood up a convert from a low caste and told what Christ had done for him. It was befitting that he should speak first, for in caste-filled India God was taking the weak things to confound the mighty, just as it was befitting that Carey the cobbler should be the first teacher of Brahman India. After him arose one who had been a Brahman Hindu and told of what he had found. Then, to our surprise, the head British official of the district arose and said: "Seven years ago I could not have said that I had found this that we have been talking about here tonight. But seven years ago I found it through an old lady, on board ship coming out to India." It was a rich testimony from a very Christian life, simply told and meaning much, for many of the men before him were his subordinate officers. Then the leading Roman Catholic layman of the city testified: "Of course I have never spoken in a meeting of this kind before, but I could not sit here and refuse to tell before my non-Christian friends what Christ is to me. I heard him say to me, 'Come unto me, all you that labor and are heavy laden, and I will give you rest.' I came. He gave me rest." It was a striking testimony. Now feel the accumulated effect of that whole thing. Here were low caste and high caste, American and English, Protestant and Catholic, telling before their Hindu friends what Christ was to them. The Hindu chairman of the meeting at the close thoughtfully said to me, "I can answer most of your arguments, but I do not know what to do with this."

There in miniature was seen what a united witness of the church would mean. Christendom is now talking in different directions—a good part of the time against others called Christians and not much about the Lord—"finding a precarious living," as someone said of the people of a certain island, "by washing each other's clothes." But suppose we should come together at the place of our common Lord and would with one joyous voice witness of him, what would happen—what? Something that would be irresistible, as it was to that Hindu chairman.

In speaking of the witness of the lips, I do not mean to overlook the fact that it must be a witness backed by life. "This man who is to speak today is back of everything he says," said the chairman of a meeting in introducing a speaker. He could have said nothing finer.

A friend of mine went into a shoe shop and found the Hindu shopkeeper in deep distress. He had lost his only son. My friend to comfort him said, "Well, my brother, remember in your trouble that God is love." The Hindu's face brightened up and he said, "Yes, I know God is love." My friend, interested at his evident eagerness, asked, "How do you know God is love?" "Oh," said the Hindu, "I worked for Foy sahib in Cawnpore, and no one could work for Foy sahib and not know God is love."[2] Here was a witness with the whole of life behind it. Forty years of beautiful living was speaking to the Hindu in his hour of distress.

Christ interpreted through experience and backed by fine living is almost irresistible to India today.

---

2. Sahib was a term of respect for Europeans used by Hindus and Muslims in colonial India and was often appended to names or titles. Cawnpore is the anglicized name of what is now Kanpur, a city in Uttar Pradesh. Foy is perhaps as reference to Arthur Foy, who had lived in Kanpur and died in 1902, or one of his descendants.

CHAPTER IX

What or Whom?

THIS Christian spirit scattered here and there in many hearts in India must express itself in some kind of corporate relationships. Some kind of a church will be the final outcome. We will put our Western corporate experience at the disposal of the forming church in India and we will say to her, "Take as much as you may find useful for your purposes but be first-hand and creative and express Christ through your own genius."

We know that this has its dangers. It might be easier to block them off as they do in orphan asylums and turn them out on a standard pattern—easier and more deadly. The German missionaries in their thoroughness have done this in their missions. In the theological seminaries the students are pumped full of truth. They go out to take charge of churches where they grind out that truth. In each church in the whole of the mission the pastors preach on the same texts, read the same lessons, and preach the same sermons. They go round the circle of truth once in three years. Then they begin over again. It was all "faultily faultless, icily regular, splendidly null."

Jesus did not do that. He gave himself to them. When they got the life, they created suitable raiment in which to clothe it. Life was more than raiment.

While we cannot tell what may be the final outcome of this expression of the Christ of the Indian Road on the part of his followers in India, we can see at this distance certain things that will be avoided and certain things gained if they center everything upon Christ.

If India keeps this vision clear, she will be saved from many of the petty divisions that have paralyzed us in great measure. For at the central place of our experience of Jesus we are one. *It is Christ who unites us; it is doctrines that divide*. As someone has suggested, if you ask a congregation of Christians, "*What* do you believe?" there will be a chorus of conflicting beliefs, for no two persons believe exactly alike. But if the question is asked, "*Whom* do you trust?" then we are together. If the emphasis in our approach to Christianity is "What?" then it is divisive, but if the emphasis is "Whom?" then we are drawn together at the place of this Central Magnet. One has the tendency of the centrifugal and the other the tendency of the centripetal. Jesus is the hub that holds together in himself the divided spokes.

The church in China has been rent by controversy. I can see reasons why this has happened. While there I was struck with the fact that Christianity was, on the whole, presented to the Chinese as good teaching, good doctrine, good national policy. It seemed to me to lack just this Christocentric emphasis to which we have been driven in India. It needed the warm touch of the personal Christ to make it tingle with life and radiance. At the Central Fire, suspicious groups could have warmed themselves and would have felt the glow of comradeship as they did so.

Christianity with a *what*-emphasis is bound to be divisive, but this tendency is lessened with a *Whom*-emphasis. Note the things that have created denominations in the West: baptism, human freedom, rites, ceremonies, church government, dress, orders—the points of division have been nearly all "whats."

The church divided once over the "Whom," namely, in the Unitarian issue. Here it had a right to divide, for the question of who Jesus is is vital and decisive. Everything is bound up with that question.

This question of who Jesus is was thrown into the very center of the church in India in recent years. One keen Indian minister's discovery of the modern method rather went to his head and landed him in a Unitarian position. He threw the whole matter into the Indian church for airing. Some of us held our breath as we watched the controversy rage back and forth in one of the papers for several years. The missionaries practically stood out of it and let the growing church come to its own conclusions as to who her Lord is. In the beginning the brother of Unitarian views had the center and held it. But gradually a change came, and when the battle was over, our brother and his views had been pushed to the margin and a divine Christ occupied the center. By the sheer force of his own Person, Jesus had shone into the situation and had clarified it. The Indian church has fought her first battle—she knows who her Lord is, not merely through what the missionaries had said, but because she had thought it through for herself. It was a living victory. At the close she knelt at his feet with a joy unknown before, saying, "My Lord and my God." This victory came not by dogmatic assertion, but by painstaking methods of careful and prayerful research.

Now, the significant thing was this, that at the end of the battle men of liberal and conservative minds had been drawn together at Him. He held them both. The problem of unity will be well on the way to solution if the Indian church makes Christ central and all else marginal.

Some of the other problems that are now vexing the mind of the West will not vex us if we keep this Christocentric emphasis. Christianity cannot be really understood with a *what*-emphasis, but it can be understood with a *Whom*-emphasis.

Take the whole question of the supernaturalness of Christianity. It claims to be a supernatural system. Now, as men's minds have discovered a universe of law this idea of a supernaturally imposed system seemed less and less credible until the attempt has been made to rationalize the whole system, explain away the miracles and reduce the whole thing to natural law. But in Christianity we are not discussing miracles in the light of natural law but in the light of the personality of Jesus, and that makes a difference—a very great one. The question is, Would miracles happen around such a personality as Jesus?

Now, we used to go at it something like this: Jesus was born in a supernatural way, he did supernatural things, he arose in a supernatural manner, therefore he was a supernatural Person. The miracles carried Jesus—the *what* carried the *Whom*. This is obviously weak. It sends the minds of men and women to the *whats*, where they wrangle over them and only incidentally get to the *Whom*. If we were wiser, we would ask men and women to lay aside the question of birth and miracle for a moment, until they get under the sway of this Person. Let them catch the force of this Mind and Soul into which no impurity had ever entered, no sin had ever marred, let them feel the touch of him upon them, and then let them turn from the standpoint of this Person to the question of miracles and they become credible in the light of what he is. In the light of natural law miracle seems absurd, but in the light of this person of Jesus it becomes the most natural of things.

I once asked Professor Hans Dreisch, the great German philosopher and exponent of "Vitalism," this question: "Whenever you get a higher type of life do you not expect that around that life there will be a higher type of manifestation?" He assented to this, and I asked him further, "If Jesus represents a higher type of being, would you not have to make room in your thinking that around that life would be a higher type of doing which to us on a lower plane might be considered miracle?" He replied: "Yes, if Jesus represents a higher type of being, I would have to make room in my thinking that around that life would be the possibility of what might seem to us on a lower plane miracle. But it would have to be examined scientifically." Precisely!

We are willing to rest everything on the question of whether or not Jesus represented a higher type of being. There is only one way to settle it: Stand before Jesus in inward moral surrender and obedience and see if you can feel that what you stand before is mere human nature. If he is human nature, then we are not—we are subhuman, for he stands above saint as well as sinner. Professor Hogg, who has companioned with this Christ of the Indian Road for many years and knows him well, puts the matter in these burning words:

> When, as detached bystanders, we look upon his features, as it were, in profile, considering them singly and in repose, we seem to find none that is not human, none at least that does not belong to the nature which God designed for man. But let us move in front and catch His glance, so that the personality which lived by means of these human endowments may pierce our consciousness with a look in which its eager passion and its tender pity, its searching purity, and its gracious comprehendingness, its assurance of a world-redeeming vocation and its unaffected neighborliness, its kingly demands and its selfless devotion, make simultaneous impact on our souls, and we shall then lose all intent to measure or to classify; we shall know ourselves in the presence of the utterly unique—One who exacts worship instead of submitting to appraisal. Merely look at Jesus, and you behold a Man. But meet him face to face in the inwardness of comradeship and obedience, of faltering need and kingly succor, and you know

> yourself to be meeting the very Person, the very Self of God. I do not explain this; I simply testify."[1]

And who that has tried it has not felt what Professor Hogg so graphically expressed?

Here is the central miracle of Christianity: Christ. The central miracle is not the resurrection or the virgin birth or any of the other miracles; the central miracle is just this Person, for he rises in sinless grandeur above life. He is life's Sinless Exception, therefore a miracle. Now, turn from that Central Miracle toward these lesser miracles and they become credible in the light of his Person. Being what he was, it would be amazing if he did not touch blind eyes and make the lame to walk. These miracles fit in with the central miracle of his Person. "Being a miracle, it would be a miracle if he did not perform miracles." The miracles do not carry Jesus—he carries them. The "whom" carries the "what," the Person carries the manifestation. But say miracle apart from him and it is confusing.

From this standpoint let us approach the vexed question of the virgin birth. Discuss "virgin birth" apart from Jesus and it seems incredible and absurd but connect it with him and it fits in with the whole and becomes credible. Let it be said at once that I do not base his divinity on how he was born. If it had been said that he was born in an ordinary way and I still saw in him what I now see in him, I would still believe in him as divine. Not *how* he came into the world, but *what* he was after he got here is the most important thing. But in the light of his Person, I see no difficulty whatever in believing in the virgin birth. Since he rose above life in sinless grandeur, it becomes possible to believe that he arose above the ordinary processes of birth. "The virgin life of Jesus makes it possible to believe in

---

1. Alfred George Hogg, *Redemption from This World* (Edinburgh, T&T Clark, 1924), 65–66.

the virgin birth of Jesus." An Arya Samajist asked me if I could produce in human history another example of the virgin birth. I replied that I could not, for I could not produce another Jesus Christ. He was the Unique, and therefore did the unique.

A converted Jew was talking to an unconverted Jew when the latter asked, "Suppose there were a son born among us and it were claimed that he was born of a virgin, would you believe it?" The converted Jew very thoughtfully replied, "I would if he were such a Son." That is the point. *He* makes it possible to believe in *it*. But the virgin birth does not carry Jesus; he carries it. When the emphasis is on the *whom* then the *how* becomes credible. But turn it the other way and it is dark and difficult.

In regard to the resurrection the same thing holds. Jesus rose above life; this makes it perfectly credible that he would rise above death. Two things take us all—sin and death. Jesus conquered the first—our own inward moral consciousness being witness. Will he conquer the second? It would be surprising if Jesus did not. I say it reverently: If Jesus did not rise from the dead, he ought to have done so. The whole thing would come out wrong if the grave had held him captive. When the broken and dispirited disciples, now radiant with a wild hope, whispered to each other, "He is arisen," they were simply echoing what his whole life had done. Throughout his life he arose. Where we sank, he arose. The resurrection fits in with that fact. There must be an empty tomb where there is such a fullness of Life. Jesus carries the resurrection.

Christianity breaks into meaning when we see Jesus. The incredible becomes the actual; the impossible becomes the patent.

Do not misunderstand me: The *whats* of Christianity are important; a body of doctrine is bound to grow up around him. We cannot do without doctrine, but I am so anxious for the purity of doctrine that I want it to be held in the white light of his Person and under the constant corrective of his living Mind. The only place where we can hold our doctrines pure is to hold them in the light of his countenance. Here their defects are at once apparent, but only here.

But we must hold in mind that no doctrine, however true, no statement, however correct, no teaching, however pure, can save a man. "We are saved by a Person and only by a Person, and, as far as I know, by only one Person," said Bishop William McDowell. Only Life can lift life. A doctor lay dying—a Christian doctor sat beside him and urged him to surrender to and have faith in Christ. The dying doctor listened in amazement. Light dawned. He joyously said, "All my life I have been bothered with *what* to believe, and now I see it is *whom* to trust." Life lifted life.

But further, we shall soon see that as we draw closer to him, we shall be closer to each other in doctrine. Suppose the essence of Christianity is in utter devotion to Jesus, and truly following him is the test of discipleship; will not such doctrine as the new birth take on new meaning? If I am to follow such as Jesus, I must be born again and born different. A new birth is a necessary beginning for this new life. And as for the doctrines of sanctification and the fullness of the Spirit, apart from him, they may become hollow cant, as they, in fact, have often become; but in the business of following Jesus they become, not maximum attainments, but minimum necessities. If I am to follow him, he will demand my all, and I shall not want to offer him less. Holiness has been preached very often until it has become a synonym for hollowness. The word has got loosed from Christ and has lost its meaning. Had it kept close to Christ, we would have preached less holiness and more of a Christ who makes men and women holy.

Surely, it is not difficult to believe in atonement when we think of Christ. Would such love as that let us go? Would he not go to the limit for us? Put all the content in the word "atonement" you can, and it still but faintly tells what Jesus would do for humanity.

As for the inspiration of the Scriptures, it takes a deepened meaning from him. Discuss the matter of the mechanics of it apart from Jesus and it often becomes a haggle but discuss it with our gaze upon him and it becomes a necessity. It was inconceivable that such a person as Jesus could have come out of an uninspired or an ordinarily inspired Book. The ideas, the conceptions, the Person is too lofty to have been conceived by human intelligence however lofty it might have been. Just as Jesus, being the miracle that he was, created miracles around him in human nature and the physical universe, so also around him would be created the miracle in human intelligence and insight, until things which "eye had not seen, nor ear heard, neither have entered into the heart of man," would be given forth to the world under the sway of that Person.

But the statement made above about Jesus coming out of an uninspired Book must be corrected a bit, for Jesus did not come out of the Book; it came out of him. It did not create him; he created it.

And since, as someone has suggested, literature can never rise higher than life—for life puts content and meaning into the literature—so you cannot get a better Book until you get a better life than the life of Jesus.

The strongest way to hold to the inspiration of the Scriptures is to hold to the Person.

We must call humanity not to loyalty to a belief but loyalty to a Person. We may be loyal to a belief and be dead spiritually, but we cannot be loyal to this Person and be other than alive spiritually. Jesus creates belief. He is the great Believer himself, and in the light of his radiant faith we cannot but believe. But we do not get Jesus from our beliefs, we get our beliefs from Jesus. And they must of necessity be under constant correction by his mind and spirit.

If some are afraid of what might happen if we were to give India Jesus without hard-and-fast systems of thought and ecclesiastical organization, lest the whole be corrupted, let our fears be allayed. Jesus is well able to take care of himself. He trusted himself to the early disciples, who were no better and no worse than the Indian people; and having got hold of him they went forth in that name with power. Having little ecclesiastical system, little body of set doctrine, they created their own forms out of the passion of love they had for him. These forms were real because they came out of the white heat of that passion. They expressed life. We believe that India will fall intensely in love with the Christ of the Indian Road, that love will turn to glad submission to him as Savior and Lord, that out of that loving submission will come a new radiant expression of him in thought and life.

We who feel that we must be steadiers of the ark must remember that Jesus can take care of himself, even in moments when there seems most to fear. He fell into the hands of his Jewish enemies—and lo, there was an atonement and a resurrection! Are we afraid to have him fall into the hands of his Indian friends? Will he be swallowed up? Never mind, he was swallowed up once before and there was a resurrection. There may be another! I only know that since he has come into India's thought and life everywhere there is the cracking of old things and the breaking up of dead forms. It looks to us as though there is a resurrection taking place now!

There is no real danger lest Jesus be lost among the many in all this, that it may end up in his being put in the Pantheon of Hinduism. Greece and Rome tried that, and the Pantheons amid which he was placed are gone—Jesus lives on. He is dynamic, disruptive, explosive like the soft tiny rootlets that rend the monuments of man's pride. Like the rootlets he quietly and unobtrusively goes down into the crannies of humanity's thinking, and lo, old forms and customs are broken up.

Absorb him? You may as well talk about the moist earth in springtime absorbing the seed! The seed absorbs it, for it is life. Jesus is Life. He will take care of himself.

"Give us Jesus," said a Hindu to me, "just Jesus. Do not be afraid that we will make a human Jesus out of him, for his divinity will shine out of its own accord."

At any rate there never was a situation in which Jesus was not Master, and never more so than when he was upon the cross, and even in the tomb. He will be Master upon the Indian Road—yes, even at the crossroads of India where rival creed and clashing thought flow at cross purposes.

"Where cross the crowded ways of life,
  Where sound the cries of race and clan
Above the noise of selfish strife,
  We hear thy voice, O Son of man."[2]

2. Frank Mason North (lyrics, 1903), "Where Cross the Crowded Ways of Life," in *The United Methodist Hymnal* (Nashville: Abingdon Press, 1990), no. 427.

CHAPTER X

Christ and the Other Faiths

AS Christ meets India and her past what is his demand?

When Islam confronted Hinduism, the demand was of absolute surrender—a complete wiping of the slate of the past and the dictates of the prophet written in its stead. It is no wonder that Hinduism withstood it, and does withstand it, for its very life and past are involved.

Does Jesus take that same attitude? Are his demands upon India the same as Mohammed's? Is the slate to be wiped clean and the past absolutely blotted out?

It must be confessed that this has often been the attitude and demand of the Christian missionary. If Christianity is more or less identified with Western civilization and presented as such, or if it is a system of church government and a more or less fixed theological system, blocked off and rigid and presented as such, then I do not see how we can escape the attitude of the Muslim. The past must be wiped out and a clean slate presented for our theological systems, our ecclesiastical organizations, and our civilization to be written in its stead.

But if our message be Christ, and Christ alone, then this does not necessarily follow. He may turn to India as he turned to Judaism and say, "I came not to destroy but to fulfill." Just as he gathered up in his own life and person everything that was fine and beautiful in Jewish teaching and past and gave it a new radiant expression, so he may do the same with India. The fact is that the words that he used would imply that, for it is a generic term: "I came not to destroy but to fulfill," it is locally applied to the Law and the Prophets, but capable of a wider application to truth found anywhere.

There is no doubt that devout Hindus who see worthwhile and beautiful things in their faith are deeply concerned as they see the decay of that faith and wonder what the future will bring. Hindus themselves frankly tell of that decay, but always with a pang. The brilliant Hindu editor of a newspaper in India said, "It is with a pang that I see Hinduism decaying and dying. . . . But I know how the Dhoms (outcastes) feel, for I myself am an outcaste." He had been outcasted on his return from foreign study and spoke out of a bitter experience.

The Hindu census commissioner of Baroda [now Vadodara] in his report of 1921 states, "Hinduism perhaps more than other faiths shows on its social side and its religious practices increasing signs of disintegration."

This open letter to M. T. Sheshagiri Aiyar, Member Legislative Assembly, who introduced legislation concerning the use of endowments to temples, appeared in *The Hindu Message,* an orthodox paper:

> I belong to the orthodox section of Hinduism. . . . I believe that you are aware that the orthodox section, though in the majority, are weak, disorganized, and voiceless. They belong to a rapidly dying race. In a generation or two at the most they will be nowhere, and reformers like your esteemed self will have a smooth way in seeking your cherished objects. It is exactly therefore you that should show some compassion toward the orthodox community and allow it to pass away without feeling agony, for chivalry does not consist in striking a fallen foe. . . . In your recent bill which has become the law of the land you have not provided for religious efficacy,

> but simply took compassion on what you consider to be the woeful position of women and have shed pious tears. Thus, you have helped to destroy the fabric of the ancient Hindu institutions. . . . Though weak, the orthodox has to live in this world until he is thoroughly exterminated, and until then he is destined to struggle for life.

That letter tells its own story.

This scene also has its own inner meaning. I was sitting in the train one day when two members of the Legislative Council for Madras began a heated conversation. One was a Brahman and the other a non-Brahman, both able men. They talked partly to me and partly at each other. I remained outwardly neutral. The non-Brahman in the midst of the argument said, "Yes, there was a time when we would wash your sacred feet and drink the water to purify ourselves, but now our eyes have been opened and we have thrown you over."

"Yes," replied the Brahman, "you have, and with it you have thrown over your religion."

"Well," shot back the other, "if this is religion, then religion be damned!"

There is no doubt that Brahmanism as a religion centering in the Brahman is being slowly undermined—very rapidly so, some would say. This feeling is at the back of the Brahman attack upon Gandhi for his anti-untouchability campaign.

A keen Hindu put the matter to me in rather vulgar but vivid language: "Christianity is increasing, and Hinduism is dying—damn it!"

When he says that Hinduism is dying it must be qualified a bit. Some of the outward practices of Hinduism are dying, but there are behind these practices some ideas that constitute the living spirit of Hinduism and have made it survive through the centuries. Caste and idolatry and Brahmanism will drop away, but there will be left what will constitute the core of the Indian heritage. It will be worth preserving. A lady in Baltimore found some seeds in the hands of an Egyptian mummy and planted them. Morning glories came up. In the hand of the mummied forms and customs of Hinduism I think there are five living seeds: (1) That the ultimate reality is spirit. (2) The sense of unity running through things. (3) That there is justice at the heart of the universe. (4) A passion for freedom. (5) The tremendous cost of the religious life. I do not believe that the world can afford to lose those five things so deeply imbedded in India's thought and life.

It is worth something that a nation is committed to the thought that the ultimate real is spirit. As Bernard Lucas says, "We of the West posit the material and infer the spiritual, but India posits the spiritual and infers the material." India is sure that the spiritual is real, but not quite sure that the material is, in any sense, a reality. Is that not an outlook on life that may have been providentially held to be loosed upon the world just at the time when materialism is so rampant and deadening? Again, is it worthwhile to preserve that sense of the unity of things? India has gone too far and has slipped into pantheism—everything God—but that will be corrected to a panentheism—everything in God. This will bring us a sense of the unity of all life. It should make a more friendly and meaningful and kindly universe. Again, is it worthwhile that India feels that at the heart of things is a strict and unfailing justice? The ironlike and heartless inhumanities that have grown up around the thought of karma will be modified and cleansed away, but this thought that strict justice is at the heart of things may tend to correct a good deal of our tendencies toward an easy forgiveness. Then the passion for inner freedom, the craving to break the thralldom of the outward and the seeming—that is a beautiful passion that has beat in the soul of India, and corrected by the passion for the freedom of others, will make a great contribution to our collective life. But above all,

India standing for the tremendous cost of the religious life, that religion demands all and holds all, will correct much of our compartmentalized and tentative religious thinking and acting. It should bring us *abandon*.

The shell of Hinduism breaks and falls away and leaves us these values. How can they be preserved? This is of vital interest to both East and West.

I do not think that they can be preserved through the old forms. They are falling away. They cannot be revived. A new mold and motive must be supplied for them: "The seat of authority must be new," says Maciver in another connection, but applicable here. "Insofar as the external sanctions fall away and cease to be determinants of men's conduct, it is no use any more herding them back to these and attempting to supply them with motives. They must attain to a new unity of life—they cannot regain the old."[1] Now where will that "new unity of life" be found?

Hindus themselves are beginning to see where it will be. Catch the significance of this scene and question. In ——— the Brahmans took absolute charge of our meetings. They sent out the notices through government *chaprasis*, or runners. They decided to have the meetings in the enclosed compound of a Hindu temple—an unheard-of place to hold a Christian meeting. It was specially decorated with streamers for the occasion. Hindu ushers ushered in the crowd and the leading Hindu of the city was the chairman of the meetings. Since there was no Christian to interpret for me they gave me a Hindu interpreter, a man of beautiful spirit and keen mind. He interpreted in a very dignified manner the first night, holding his hands on his

1. R. M. Maciver, *Community, a Sociological Study: Being an Attempt to Set Out the Nature and Fundamental Laws of Social Life*, 3rd ed. (New York: Macmillan, 1924), 312. The first part of the quotation here ("The seat of authority must be new") appears to be from H. R. Mackintosh, *The Originality of the Christian Message* (New York: Charles Scribner's Sons, 1920), 17. Mackintosh quotes the same passage from Maciver but introduces it with those words.

cane in front of him, but the second night he so caught the spirit of things that he began gesticulating exactly as I was doing! When I was about halfway through my address the first night the temple bells began to ring and the conch shells to blow for evening worship. As the temple was within a few feet of us there was a terrible racket. I could scarcely hear myself talk. I stood there nonplussed, when a Hindu gentleman arose and said: "Sir, just sit down. It will all be over in ten minutes; we will sit here and wait." I sat down. Not a half dozen people of that great crowd went into the temple. They sat and waited. It was all over in five or six minutes, and I resumed as though nothing had happened. The next night I spoke on the "Universality of Jesus." At the close, a Hindu lawyer arose and asked this question: "Don't you think that Hinduism will gradually evolve and change into Christianity without losing its good points?" I assured him that I thought that very thing was taking place! He saw that there was a constant drift away from the old and he was anxious that its good points should be preserved. I could assure him from my heart that Jesus came not to destroy that good, but to preserve it. This new unity of life that India must have—is it Christ? It is.

A leading Hindu lawyer of Madras expressed his belief in that conclusion in these words: "The reinvigoration of Hinduism is only possible through the Christ spirit." A Hindu High Court judge put it even more pointedly: "Christ is the only hope of Hinduism."

Would these ideas that form the finest things in India's past find new life should they die into Christianity? Would they be expressed in a new living way? Would Christ be the new mold and motive?

I believe that "these divine ideas which had wandered through the world until they had almost forgot their divine origin will at last clothe themselves in flesh and blood, the idea and the fact will meet together and will be wedded henceforth and forevermore." Jesus is that flesh and blood in which they will reclothe themselves, and that Fact in which the ideas will find living expression.

The role of the iconoclast is easy, but the role of the one who carefully gathers up in himself all spiritual and moral values in the past worth preserving is infinitely more difficult and infinitely more valuable. Hence, we can go to the East and thank God for the fine things we may find there, believing that they are the very footprints of God. He has been there before us. Everywhere that the mind of man has been open, through the crevices of that mind the light of God has shone in. That scattered light which lighted every person that came into the world was focused in the person of Jesus, and the Life became the Light of humanity.

To see how Jesus remarkably fulfills the finest striving of both East and West note the ends of life discovered by the Greeks and those discovered by the Hindus and the announcement that Jesus made about himself. The Greeks were the brain of Europe and did its philosophic thinking, just as the Hindus are the brain of Asia and have done the philosophic thinking for Asia. The Greeks said the ends of life were three: the Good, the True, and the Beautiful. The Hindus also say the ends of life are three: Gyana, Bhakti, and Karma. With this difference that the Hindus were the more religious people and made these ends means—the end was Brahma, the means to attain that were the three ways: the Gyana Marga, the way of knowledge; the Bhakti Marga, the way of devotion or emotion; the Karma Marga, the way of works or deeds.

Jesus stood between the Greeks and the Hindus, midway between East and West, and made this announcement, "I am the Way, the Truth, and the Life." Turning toward the Greeks he says, "I am the Way"—a method of acting—the Greek's Good; "I am the Truth"—the Greek's True; "I am the Life"—the Greek's Beautiful, for Life is beauty—plus. Turning toward the

Hindus he says, "I am the Way"—the Karma Marga, a method of acting; "I am the Truth"—the Gyana Marga—the method of knowing; "I am the Life"—the Bhakti Marga—the method of emotion, for Life is emotion—plus.

Jesus thus says: "I am the Good, the Beautiful, and the True; I am Gyana, Bhakti, and Karma, for I am the Way, the Truth, and the Life."

The Greeks' ends were only beautiful ideas before Jesus made them fact. "Ideas are poor ghosts," says George Eliot, "until they become incarnate." Then they look out at us from sad eyes and touch us with strong hands; then they become a power. Only as the Word becomes flesh does it move us. "The Universal Beauty must create a picture before I can say, I see. Universal Goodness must perform an action before I can say, I love. Universal Truth must have a biography before I can say, I understand."[2] Jesus is that Universal Beauty become a Picture, that Universal Goodness become an Act, that Universal Truth become a Biography. Jesus is the concrete universal.

The Gyana Marga is devotion to an Idea; the Karma Marga is devotion to a Code; the Bhakti Marga is devotion to a Person. Jesus is that Idea become a Fact, the code is now a Character, the person, the Supreme Person.

But Jesus not only faces the Greeks and the Hindus; he faces human personality everywhere and fulfills it. The modern thinker analyzes personality into Intellect, Feeling, and Will. Jesus says: "I am the Way"—here is the response of the Will; "I am the Truth"—here is the response of the Intellect; "I am the Life"—here is the response of the Feeling. Jesus is the great "Amen," the great "Yes" to human personality. He is its fulfillment since he is the Supreme Person.

But more, Jesus faces all thought and culture of all ages of the world and says, "I am the Way"—that is Ethics; "I am the

2. G. A. Studdert Kennedy, *The Wicket Gate, or, Plain Bread* (New York: George H. Doran, 1923), 82.

Truth"—that is Philosophy; "I am the Life"—that is Religion. Jesus is Ethics, Philosophy, and Religion, for he is Life, and Life includes all these and overflows them. He is the Word that sums up all other words.

But someone objects—then all these things were here before him. There was nothing new in him. H. R. Mackintosh tells of an antiquarian who shows his friend how one by one the characteristic features of Greek sculpture had been anticipated by the Assyrians, the Hittites, and the Egyptians, and he exclaimed in triumph that the Greeks had, in fact, invented nothing. "Nothing," rejoined the other, "except the Beautiful." Jesus invented nothing new. He himself was the new.

CHAPTER XI

THE CONCRETE CHRIST

INDIA is the land of mysticism. You feel it in the very air. Jesus was the supreme mystic. The Unseen was the real to him. He spent all night in prayer and communion with the Father. He lived in God and God lived in him. When he said, "I and the Father are one" (John 10:30) you feel it is so.

Jesus the mystic appeals to India, the land of mysticism. But Jesus the mystic was amazingly concrete and practical. Into an atmosphere filled with speculation and wordy disputation where "men are often drunk with the wine of their own wordiness" he brings the refreshing sense of practical reality. He taught, but he did not speculate. He never used such words as "perhaps," "may be," "I think so." Even his words had a concrete feeling about them. They fell upon the soul with the authority of certainty.

He did not discourse on the sacredness of motherhood—he suckled as a babe at his mother's breast, and that scene has forever consecrated motherhood.

He did not argue that life was a growth and character an attainment—he "grew in wisdom and stature, and in favor with God and men" (Luke 2:52).

He did not speculate on why temptation should be in this world—he met it, and after forty days' struggle with it in the wilderness he conquered, and "returned in the power of the Spirit to Galilee" (Luke 4:14).

He did not discourse on the dignity of labor—he worked at a carpenter's bench and his hands were hard with the toil of making yokes and plows, and this forever makes the toil of the hands honorable.

We do not find him discoursing on the necessity of letting one's light shine at home among kinsmen and friends—he announced his program of uplift and healing at Nazareth, his own home, and those who heard "wondered at the words of grace which proceeded out of his mouth" (Luke 4:22).

As he came among humanity, he did not try to prove the existence of God—he brought God. He lived in God, and men and women looking upon his face could not find it within themselves to doubt God.

He did not argue, as Socrates, the immortality of the soul—he raised the dead.

He did not speculate on how God was a Trinity—he said, "If I by the Spirit of God cast out devils, the kingdom of God is come nigh unto you" (Luke 10:9). Here the Trinity—"I," "Spirit of God" "God"—was not something to be speculated about but was a Working Force for redemption—the casting out of the devils and the bringing in of the Kingdom.

He did not teach in a didactic way about the worth of children—he put his hands upon them and blessed them and setting one in their midst tersely said, "Of such is the kingdom of God" (Luke 18:16) and he raised them from the dead.

He did not argue that God answers prayer—he prayed, sometimes all night, and in the morning "the power of the Lord was present to heal" (Luke 5:17).

He did not paint in glowing colors the beauties of friendship and the need for human sympathy—he wept at the grave of his friend.

He did not argue the worth of womanhood and the necessity for giving them equal rights—he treated them with infinite respect, gave to them his most sublime teaching, and when he rose from the dead he appeared first to a woman.

He did not teach in the schoolroom manner the necessity of humility—he "girded himself with a towel and kneeled down and washed his disciples' feet" (John 10:4-5).

He did not discuss the question of the worth of personality as we do today—he loved and served persons.

He did not discourse on the equal worth of personality—he went to the poor and outcast and ate with them.

He did not prove how pain and sorrow in the universe could be compatible with the love of God—he took on himself at the cross everything that spoke against the love of God, and through that pain and tragedy and sin showed the very love of God.

He did not discourse on how the weakest human material can be transformed and made to contribute to the welfare of the world—he called to him a set of weak men, as the Galilean fishermen, transformed them and sent them out to begin the mightiest movement for uplift and redemption the world has ever seen.

He wrote no books—only once are we told that he wrote and that was in the sand—but he wrote upon the hearts and consciences of people about him, and it has become the world's most precious writing.

He did not paint a Utopia, far off and unrealizable—he announced that the kingdom of heaven is within us and is "at hand" and can be realized here and now.

John sent to him from the prison and asked whether he was the one who was to come, or should they look for another? Jesus did not argue the question with the disciples of John—he simply and quietly said, "Go tell John what you see, the blind receive sight, the deaf hear, the lame walk, and the poor have the gospel preached to them" (Matthew 11:4-5). His arguments were the facts produced.

He did not discourse on the beauty of love—he loved.

We do not find him arguing that the spiritual life should conquer matter—he walked on the water.

He greatly felt the pressing necessity of the physical needs of the people around him, but he did not merely speak in their behalf—he fed five thousand people with five loaves and two fishes.

They bring in to him a man with a double malady—sick in body and stricken more deeply in his conscience because of sin. Jesus attended first of all to the deepest malady and said, "Thy sins are forgiven thee" (Matthew 9:2). In answer to the objections of the people he said, "Which is easier to say, Thy sins are forgiven thee? or to say, Take up your bed and walk? And that they might know that the Son of man had power on earth to forgive sins, he said to the palsied man, Take up your bed and walk" (9:5-6). The outward concrete miracle was the pledge of the inward.

Jesus has been called the Son of Fact. We find striking illustration of his concreteness at the Judgment seat. To those on the right he does not say, "You believed in me and my doctrines, therefore, come, be welcome into my kingdom." Instead, he said, "I was an hungered and you gave me food; I was athirst, and you gave me drink; I was sick, and you visited me; in prison, and you came unto me; a stranger, and you took me in; naked, and you clothed me" (Matthew 25:35-36). These "sons of fact," true followers of his, were unwilling to obtain heaven through a possible mistake and so they objected and said, "When saw we thee an hungered and fed thee, thirsty and gave thee drink, sick and visited thee?" (25:44) and the Master answered, "Inasmuch as ye did it to one of the least of these ye did it unto me" (25:45). He was not only concrete himself, he demanded a concrete life from those who were his followers.

He told us that the human soul was worth more than the whole material universe, and when he had crossed a storm-tossed lake to find a storm-tossed soul, ridden with devils, he did not hesitate to sacrifice the two thousand swine to save this one lost man.

He did not argue the possibility of sinlessness he presented himself and said, "Which of you convinceth me of sin?" (John 8:46).

He did not merely ask humanity to turn the other cheek when smitten on the one, to go the second mile when compelled to go one, to give the cloak also when sued at the law and the coat was taken away, to love our enemies and to bless them—he himself did that very thing. The servants struck him on one cheek, he turned the other and the soldiers struck him on that; they compelled him to go with them one mile—from Gethsemane to the judgment hall—he went with them two—even to Calvary. They took away his coat at the judgment hall and he gave them his seamless robe at the cross; and in the agony of the cruel torture of the cross he prayed for his enemies, "Father, forgive them, for they know not what they do" (Luke 23:34).

He did not merely tell us that death need have no terror for us—he rose from the dead, and lo, now the tomb glows with light.

Many teachers of the world have tried to explain everything—they changed little or nothing. Jesus explained little and changed everything.

Many teachers have tried to diagnose the disease of humanity—Jesus cures it.

Many teachers have told us why the patient is suffering and that he should bear with fortitude—Jesus tells him to take up his bed and walk.

Many philosophers speculate on how evil entered the world—Jesus presents himself as the way by which it shall leave.

He did not go into long discussions about the Way to God and the possibility of finding him—he quietly said to men and women, "I am the Way" (John 14:6).

Many speculate with Pilate and ask, "What is truth?" Jesus shows himself and says, "I am the Truth."

Herbert Spencer defines physical life for us—Jesus defines life itself, by presenting himself and saying, "I am the Life." Anyone who truly looks upon him knows in the inmost depths of his soul that he is looking on Life itself.

There is no deeper need in India and the world today than just this practical mysticism that Jesus brings to bear upon the problems of life. "No man is strong who does not bear within himself antitheses strongly marked." The merely mystical human is weak, and the merely practical human is weak, but Jesus the practical Mystic, glowing with God and yet stooping in loving service to humanity, is Strength Incarnate.

It is no wonder that India, tired of speculation, turns unconsciously toward him, the mystic Servant of all.

CHAPTER XII

THE INDIAN INTERPRETATION OF JESUS

THE answer to the question as to what will be the distinctive notes in the interpretation of Christ through Indian genius and bent can be given only tentatively. That answer can only be left with India. But that there will be a distinctive note is certain.

The Christian Church in its sanest and most spiritual times has fixed upon the person of Jesus as the center and real essential of Christianity. But as his teaching and life goes through each national genius it receives a tinge from the life through which it passes. Paul speaks of "my gospel." It was a gospel that had gone through the thinking and mentality of a man deeply soaked in Judaism. He poured the richness of that gospel through those modes of thinking. Paul could truly say, "It is my gospel," for no one else could give exactly that same expression of Christianity that Paul could give, since no one else had the same social inheritance through which to express it.

When Christianity went further and touched the brain of Europe in Greece, it received another expression. As we look back to Christianity, we largely see it through "the binocular of Greek metaphysics and Roman law." Greece did the thinking for Europe, and it was in this atmosphere that some of our creeds were formed. Someone has said that at Pentecost everyone heard the gospel in his own tongue, but at Nicaea the voice was Greek. We are deeply grateful for that voice and for those creeds. They have kept Christianity very often from drifting into a meaningless tolerant theosophy. Thomas Carlyle taunted Christendom that it had been divided over a diphthong, but later he acknowledged that the whole of Christianity was probably bound up in the question of that diphthong. This preciseness of Greek intellect has been a mighty steadying force as Christianity has gone on its way. But it has by that very preciseness helped to stereotype Christianity in certain mental forms. As Christianity went through the Romans many of the theories of the atonement were largely taken out of forms found in Roman law. When we read of some of those discussions on the atonement we feel the legal atmosphere—God is the Judge, men and women are mere subjects, the universe has law written in it and the relationship between God and humanity is a legal relationship. Certainly, it is a great gain thus to have an orderly universe and the thought of iron law at the center of things. But though it had received this contribution, Christianity found itself cramped in the Roman legal forms, even crippled. God is more than law; God is love expressing himself through law. The world is not a courtroom, but a family; and the relationship between God and man is not a legal one of ruler and subject, but a filial one between Father and son. Our inheritance from both Greek and Roman has helped and yet seriously hindered.

The Anglo-Saxon inheritance has deeply influenced Christianity. MacDougall reminds us that the Norsemen, the ancestors of the Anglo-Saxon people, dwelt on the rugged coastline of Norway. They got most of their living from the sea, but it was not sufficient, so they cultivated those rugged hillsides. It was a precarious existence and could sustain only a limited number of persons. When the sons came on, they were compelled to launch out for themselves, for the hillsides could not sustain them. Hence, they went to distant lands and conquered and settled. Out of this social inheritance came three great characteristics: self-reliance, aggressiveness, and the love of individual freedom. Each family became self-sufficient through its own self-reliance and depended little on the settled community.

Those three characteristics are among the Anglo-Saxons today. Christianity coming in contact with this social inheritance has been expressed largely in terms of self-reliance, aggressiveness, and individual freedom. An Englishman speaking before an audience said, "I trust I am a Christian Englishman, but I cannot help but remember that I am an *English* Christian and that my life has been molded by the teachings of the New Testament and by contemporaneous English society." The forms of expression of Christianity in Anglo-Saxon lands have been largely individualistic and aggressive. This is certainly an inheritance that has enriched, but it has also given only a partial expression of Christianity and has lacked those deep social meanings and social expressions which lie at the heart of Christianity. Protestantism with its love of individual liberty flourished in this atmosphere. But as someone has said, "Protestantism in breaking up the idea of a universal church came near losing the idea of our universal humanity." We are just now trying to counteract that bad effect by the message of the social application of the gospel.

America is also giving us a type of Christianity that loves such words as "pep," "snappiness," and "accomplishment." The race question has also determined some of the forms that Christianity has taken in America. In a certain place in America, the black and the white people had a union service. At the close a lady on her return home said, "It was all very nice and all very Christian, but if we are to be Christian in our churches what is it going to lead to?" Here was Christianity trying to break through a social inheritance and express itself in universal terms but caught and cramped by a social inheritance that practically forbade universality.

The religious genius of India is the richest in the world, the forms that it has taken have often been the most extravagant, sometimes degrading, and cruel. These forms are falling away, or will fall away, but the spirit persists and will be poured through other forms. As that genius pours itself through Christian molds it will enrich the collective expression of Christianity. But in order to do that the Indian must remain Indian. The Indian must stand in the stream of India's culture and life and let the force of that stream go through his soul so that the expression of Indian Christianity will be essentially Eastern and not Western. This does not mean that Indian Christianity will be denied what is best in Western thought and life, for when firmly planted on its own soil it can then lift its antennae to the heavens and catch the voices of the world. But it must be particular before it can be universal. Only thus will it be creative—a voice, not an echo.

Someone writing to me on the subject said, "The first thing necessary is to create a live Indian"—a man alive to his past, his possibilities, his religious genius. Given that spirit, Indian Christianity will find its own forms as the day follows the night.

The reason that the Indian Christian has not made any real contribution to Christian theology is because he has been trying, on the whole, to think through Western forms, and here he is like a fish out of water. But now that India is awakened and self-conscious and the process of denationalization is probably over, we may expect that genius to work. We must be willing to trust Indians to make their contribution.

It is no more fair to say that we cannot trust Indian genius to interpret Christianity because of the extravagances of the past than to have said that the Western mind could not be trusted because the Druids in England used to perform human sacrifices in their religion and the Scots practiced cannibalism.

Every nation has its peculiar contribution to make to the interpretation of Christianity. The Son of man is too great to be expressed by any one portion of humanity. Those that differ from us most will probably contribute most to our expression of Christianity.

Here is the inward feeling of a patriotic Slavic person as to the contribution of his race. In a personal letter written to Professor H. A. Miller more than a year before the war by a Bohemian who for thirty years had been a professor of German in a German Gymnasium, he unburdens his hopes for his people thus: "I am not pessimistic enough to give up all hopes that Providence may have some good things in store for the Slavs. What keeps me up is a certain hazy impression that human development may some time be in want of a new formula, and then our time may come. I conceive ourselves under the sway of the German watchword which spells 'force,' and as watchwords come and go, like everything else human, perhaps the Slav may some time be called on to introduce another, which I would like to see spelled 'Charity.'"[1]

India too hopes that the world may someday be in need of a new formula. She too has her word ready. It will be spelled "Atma"—*spirit*. That word "Atma" runs like a refrain through everything in India. The followers of the Christ of the Indian Road will show us the real meaning of a *spiritual* life. They will sit lightly to earthly things and abandon themselves to the spirit.

Along with that will come the sense of the unity and harmony running through things. "Don't you think atonement would mean attunement?" said a Hindu to me one day. He felt his life was "like sweet bells jangled out of tune" by sin and evil, and to his mind, craving inward peace and harmony,

1. Herbert Adolphus Miller, *Races, Nations, and Classes: The Psychology of Domination and Freedom* (Philadelphia: J. B. Lippincott, 1924), 82.

atonement would bring attunement to the nature of God—music instead of a discord. No wonder peace has been the great thought and craving of India. Anything like losing one's temper is thought to be utterly incompatible with the truly religious life. "I know I haven't salvation yet" said a villager to me one day, "for while I have conquered everything else, anger still remains, I haven't got it yet." The followers of the Christ of the Indian Road will be harmonized and peaceful. Meditation to them will be real. Religion will mean quiet realization. God will be the harmonizing bond of all.

Finally, the followers of the Christ of the Indian Road will know the meaning of the cross, for India stands for the cost of being religious. Renunciation will be a reality, for India instinctively grasps the meaning of Jesus when he says that the way to realize life is to renounce it—to lose it is to find it. In the footprints of many of his followers as they walk along the Indian Road will be blood stains, for they will be Apostles of the Bleeding Feet. They will know the meaning of being crucified followers of a crucified Lord.

There is a term and conception that sums up these ideas and gives them vital expression—a term that is deeply imbedded in India's thought and practice, namely, "Bhakti." It means faith, and yet more than faith, it means devotion, and yet is deeper than devotion; it expresses following another, and yet is richer than that. It means Self committed to Another—an utter self-abandonment, until that Other becomes the life of our life, the very center of our being. The lesser life is transformed into the moral and spiritual image of the Object of the Bhakti and draws its very life from the Other. I say "Object," but that sounds too distant for this relation, for here Subject and Object almost cease to be, for Life follows into life, Being into being.

This was doubtless Paul's conception of faith, but the word has lost some of its deep original meanings and has become more or less identified with belief or trust. Self-committal is not its principal content. India will restore this through Bhakti.

But in taking Bhakti from India, Christianity will broaden and enrich it. With India, Bhakti has had its center in the emotions. In Christ, it will be in the whole person. For Christ brings life to the whole of life.

Now, we believe God to be personal—not corporeal, but personal. In personality there are at least three things, grounded in a fourth—intellect, feeling and will—these grounded in self-consciousness. We too are personal—we have those four things. Now, religion is the response of my personality to the personality of God. Religion means, then, that I would think God's thoughts after him, feel his feelings after him, will his purposes after him and become his being after him. But apart from Jesus I know little of God, so religion means to me to think Christ's thoughts, feel his feelings, will his purposes, and become his being.

Christianity uses ritual, but it is not ritual; it has beliefs, but it is not a belief; it has institutions, but it is not an institution. In its deepest meaning it is person giving itself to Person, life to Life.

Jesus said that Bhakti was to be of the whole man: "Thou shalt love the Lord thy God with all thy heart [the feeling nature], with all thy mind [the intellectual nature], with all thy soul [the volitional nature], and with all thy strength [the physical nature]" (Matthew 22:37). The whole man, including the physical, is to be brought under the sway of God. But with all thy strength would go further than the strength of the physical—it would mean the strength of the mind, the strength of the feeling, the strength of the will. Many are loving God in an unbalanced and unsymmetrical way and, therefore, weak way. They love him with the strength of the feeling and the weakness of the mind—that makes the emotionalist in religion; some love him with the strength of the emotions and the weakness of the will—that makes the sentimentalist in religion; others love him with the strength of the mind and the weakness of the emotions—the mere intellectualist in religion; others love him with the strength of the will and the weakness of the emotions—this produces the man of iron, very moral, but unlovely and unlovable. The really strong Christian is one that loves with the strength of the mind, the strength of the emotions, the strength of the will—the strength of the whole personality—the entire being caught up in a passion of love and self-surrender to Christ. As Christ gives all, he claims all.

So, the Christian Bhakta or devotee will practice neither the asceticism of the mind, nor of the feeling, nor of the will—not asceticism but consecration; not drying up but development; self-renunciation in order to self-development. The soul thus becomes like a well-directed sailboat—a directing mind guiding the rudder (the will) and with the sails (the emotions) filled with the winds of heaven. The whole of life will go ahead and progress.

"Bhakti" is a beautiful and rich term and broadened by the original Christian conception should enrich our expression of Christianity.

When I think of the type that sums up these realities and gives us a sample of a really Indian expression of Christianity, I think of Sadhu Sundar Singh. In his besandaled feet, his long flowing yellow robe, in his lack of earthly possessions, in the quiet calm and joy of his face, he looks as though he had just stepped out of the pages of the New Testament. Here is Christianity going through a truly Indian spirit, and the world bends over to catch the music of it. When Sadhu Sundar Singh goes to Europe there are no halls or churches large enough to hold the crowds in large university centers. As they listen, they catch the accents that amid the complexity of our civilization sound new life that has caught the meaning of the supremacy and reality of the spirit, that knows harmony and peace and is utterly abandoned to the Christ of the Indian Road.

As someone has said, "The final commentary on the Gospels cannot be written until India has been Christianized."

CHAPTER XIII

THE CHRIST OF THE INDIAN ROAD

SOME time ago I was criticized kindly but earnestly by a missionary in India who complained that "I preached a living Christ instead of a dead Christ." I think I knew what he meant. He felt I did not enough emphasize what Jesus did, expressed in fixed formulas and set systems, not enough of that once-and-for-all-accomplished idea. I pleaded guilty, though I could say with my brother that I thought I could go as far as he went—maybe further—in believing in what Jesus accomplished for us upon the cross. He died for me. Fill those words with all the wealth of meaning that grateful human hearts can put into them, and I still feel there is room for something else to be said. Jesus was the *Unspeakable Gift*. I weave my formulas about him, and he steps out beyond them! The Word is too big for my words. But I believe in that past. Jesus is the same yesterday. Cut the historical from the experiential and there will soon be no experiential. We must have the past.

Yet Christ is living today. He not only accomplishes for us in the past, he accompanies us in the present. He is no spent force. He is the Great Contemporary. Studdart Kennedy is right when he says that we do not know what it is that is troubling us in our modern world, but that it is this: Christ has got hold of us. We are not nearly as smugly complacent as we were. We cannot bring ourselves to obey him absolutely or to turn away from him. He is getting hold of us in the East and West.

I find him in places and movements I had never dreamed of and by the quiet sense of his presence he is forcing modification everywhere. Call the roll of the reforms that are sweeping across India, and whether they be economic, social, moral, or religious, they are all tending straight toward Christ and his thought. Not one of them is going away from him, that is, if it be a reform and not a reaction.

A friend, in describing Sir George Gabriel Stokes, the discoverer of the science of spectroscopy and the theory of the undulation of light, told me of how very gentle and retiring he was. Along with this modesty he was a saint. He did not care a scrap if people did not recognize him as the author of these discoveries. He was constantly behind Kelvin and Thomson and others pushing them forward while he remained unnoticed. "I cannot tell you," he concluded, "how many things he was behind." As we sat there, we talked of how many things Jesus was behind in India and the East, though often unnoticed.

A Cabinet minister in Japan, in reply to the question, "How do you account for the immense increase of labor unrest since the war?" instead of attributing it to Bolshevism, said, "It is Christianity working among the people; the working man is testing Christ's preaching of larger life and freedom." As a non-Christian laborer put it to one of our missionaries: "We laborers understand Christ, for he was a laboring man and bore a cross. Every laborer understands that cross, for he has to bear one." Back of many of the movements throughout the East, the living Spirit of Jesus can be felt.

The last Muslim king of Oudh had 365 wives. One of his palaces has now been turned into a Legislative Council Hall. I sat there in that former harem and listened to a debate on woman's suffrage and saw Hindus and Muslims pass the bill unanimously. Up in the galleries was a fine group of our splendidly trained and educated young women of the Isabella Thoburn College. Again and again the speakers referred to their presence and one of them said, "We've got to give them suffrage—see who are looking down on us." Without a word there was the silent pressure of the Christian spirit upon the situation. Jesus was back of it.

Travancore [now a part of Kerala] is the most caste-ridden section of India. Yet in the very center of it we sat down to an intercaste dinner—a hundred high-caste Hindus, a hundred outcastes, a hundred Indian Christians, a few Muslims, and several of us of the West. They mixed us up so that here was a high caste, next to him an outcaste, a Muslim, one of us, an outcaste again, and so on down the line. I sat between a Muslim and an outcaste. As I sat down the Muslim said, "Well, thank God we are all down together at last." As I sat there and watched the amazed faces of those outcastes, faces that bore the marks of the centuries of suppression, I thought I saw One standing back of them saying, "I was in prison and you visited me" (Matthew 25:36). The chains of the centuries were being broken by the pressure of the Spirit of the Son of man upon the conscience.

By the silent pressure of his presence Jesus is forcing modification everywhere. Movements are springing up, many of them but dimly recognizing that the impelling Spirit of Jesus is behind them. "Hindu Christians!" said a discerning Hindu with a smile to me as we watched a crowd of earnest Hindu social workers. Christ is abroad upon the Indian Road, and as he sits by the wayside the sensitive soul of India knows that he understands toil and pain and sorrow and enters in and feels with them. One of the leading Hindu thinkers of North India at the close of my address expressed the truth in these beautiful words: "The thing that strikes me about Jesus is his imaginative sympathy. He entered into the experiences of humanity and felt with them. He could feel the darkness of the blind, the leprosy of the leper, the loneliness of the rich, the degradation of the poor, and the guilt of the sinner. And who shall we say he is? He called himself the Son of man. He also called himself the Son of God—we must leave it at that." This professor beautifully expressed what men are vaguely feeling.

Jesus does not stand before the blind and the leper and the poor and the sinner and discourse philosophically on why they are in such condition but lays his hands of sympathy upon them and heals them through his servants; and more—he puts his gentle but condemning finger upon the conscience of the hale and hearty Pharisee in the crowd and asks why he has allowed all this. "Why?" he persists in asking. And for the first time people begin to feel that they are in very truth their brother's keeper, and that the wretchedness of the poor and the sick is not a sign of their sin of a previous birth, but the sign of the sin of the privileged in this birth for allowing it. Movements come out of such thoughts as these, and such thoughts are coming from Christ, very often standing unnoticed in the shadows.

Some do recognize what is happening. The Hindu professor of modern history in a South India college said to me, "My study of modern history has shown me that there is a Moral Pivot in the world today, and that the best life of both East and West is more and more revolving about that center—that Moral Pivot is the person of Jesus Christ." It is as interesting as a novel to watch humanity's thoughts and spirits as they get within the sphere of his influence, being caught by the attraction of his person and their life beginning to revolve about him. This is the sphere of influence that we watch with bated breath. All other spheres of influence in the East created for purposes of exploitation and political intrigue are the breeding places for jealousy and strife, but this sphere of influence of Jesus is healing and cementing and saving.

Listen to the testimony of this outstanding philosopher of India, a man deeply read in the philosophy of East and West. When I asked him my question, I inwardly steeled myself for the shock of his criticism, for I knew it would be keen. "Professor, what do you think of Jesus Christ?" I asked. He replied: "We had high ideas of God before Jesus came. But Jesus is the highest expression of God that we have seen. He is conquering us by the sheer force of his own person even against our wills." Jesus wins, not because of any religious trick or cleverness, but because he is winsome; he compels, not because he calls in Cæsar's help, but because he is compelling; he is Savior just because men and women find in him what a Savior ought to be—he saves; he draws the world just by being lifted up.

Christ is confronting men and women everywhere. He has got hold of us. A Hindu lawyer of fine ability gave an address to which I listened on the topic, "The Inescapable Christ." He said: "We have not been able to escape him. There was a time when our hearts were bitter and sore against him, but he is melting them by his own winsomeness. Jesus is slowly but surely entering all men in India—yea, all men." The only thing that I could think of all through the address was this: "Other sheep I have, which are not of this fold. Them also I must bring" (John 10:6). How is it possible to limit or demarcate the lines of the Kingdom anymore? Jesus steps beyond them, and shocked and frightened like the Pharisees of other days we stand and wonder how far he will go in his warm sympathy and understanding. He eats with publicans and sinners and with the Hindu too. No wonder H. G. Wells in summing up the influence of Jesus upon human history in his *Outline of History* exclaims, "The Galilean has been too great for our small hearts."[1]

1. H. G. Wells, *The Outline of History*, 3rd ed. (New York: Macmillan, 1922), 505. The quotation from Wells is slightly different: "Is it any wonder that to this day this Galilean is too much for our small hearts?"

When this Galilean was upon earth with us, he said of the outside Gentile's faith, "I have not found so great faith even in Israel." He must be saying the same thing again, for the "outside" world surprises us again. I talked in Hindi with a Sadhu one day. In the midst of the conversation, he broke out into the purest English, and pulling a New Testament from under his cloak, he said, "This is my meat and drink."

"But" I said, rather taken aback, "you are connected with this temple, what are you doing with that?"

"Yes," he said, and then repeated, "It is my meat and drink."

When I asked him what he thought of it he eagerly replied: "All other religions are passing away or will pass away; Jesus alone will remain."

Is the faith of the Sadhu being realized? Are other things passing away and is Jesus beginning to fill the horizon? I know it is easy in a matter of this kind to overdraw the picture, to read into the situation what one would like to see, but in the narrative of this little book I have let the testimony of Hindus tell the story. If it is overdrawn, they have overdrawn it. But the facts themselves tell me that the Sadhu is right.

Jesus is forcing modification everywhere. He stands unmodified. In all this battle and struggle of things—and Jesus hasn't won this place in the soul of India without his Calvarys of misunderstanding and abuse, and there are more to come—nevertheless, in this clash of ideas and ideals we have not been called upon to modify a single thing about him. We are called upon, with deep insistence, to modify our civilization, our church, ourselves—everything, except him. A Hindu principal of a college said to me, "Your trouble is with the Christian Church." Even so, but that is remediable. We can remedy our church, our civilization, ourselves. But suppose he had been able to say, "Your trouble is with your Christ"—that would be irremediable; it would be fatal. "Smite the shepherd, and the sheep will be scattered abroad." Smite Jesus with a legitimate moral or spiritual criticism, and we are worse than scattered abroad. We are done for. But I say the literal truth when I say that people are not asking for modification there; the demand is for interpretation and imitation.

Jesus walks along the roads of India's thought and life, and everywhere there is a new sense of values, a new feeling that there is healing in the air, a new sense that there is a spring-time of the soul upon us as the old frozen forms of life break up and melt and there are stirrings of new life all around, a new hope—a regenerating Presence has come. I had baptized a group of outcastes in their section of the village. At the close of the ceremony the father of the house took me by the hand and said, "Sir, I want you to walk through my compound and through my little house, and when you have passed through all the impurities and sin of our past will be taken away and all will be purified." I marveled at his simple faith in me and shrank from its implications. But I was grateful that I did know One who was walking along the highways of India, through her compounds, into her lowly cottages and through the bazaars, and everywhere he goes there is a new sense of purity, a new feeling of the worthwhileness of life, a new eagerness to serve—there is renewal, regeneration.

"We have met Christ today, haven't we?" said a Sadhu with a shining face, as he was leaving my room. Yes, *we* had.

It is India's day of meeting Christ—and ours. In their meeting him, we too have met him.

As I have sat writing the experiences of these seventeen years two simple incidents have kept recurring again and again. They were so simple that they should have faded with the moment, but while the introductory statements of chairmen of our meetings have been forgotten, these two things persist, and in their persisting bless. A little Indian girl of about seven years was playing around the bungalow with our little girl. I was seated on the veranda at my writing. As they darted past me, the little Indian girl paused, and in her shy way came up to me, passed her little brown hand across my cheek and said, *"Apke munh mujhe bahut piyara lagta"*—"Your face is very dear to me." As she ran on, I brushed away a tear and went on with my writing. But my heart was very warm. As I have sat writing this book here in America, I have felt again the soft touch of India's hand upon my cheek, and my heart has been warm, for India has become very dear to me. But I find that my love for India has a quality in it now that it did not have in the early days. I went to India through pity, I stay through respect. I love India because she is lovable, I respect her because she is respectable; she has become dear to me because she is endearing.

The other occurred when I was in Shantineketan at the Ashram of Tagore. I sat on the edge of the steps and watched the temple service one day. At the close a student went forward, took a lotus flower—the national flower of India—from a bowl upon the table in front, came back and presented it to me. As I arose to receive it, he bent and touched my feet, as is the custom with their gurus, or teachers. It was done very simply and very beautifully. I had come there a stranger and a foreigner, I had come openly with another faith, and I wondered how I would be received, but when this student gave me this lotus flower before all, then I knew I was accepted as friend and brother—and teacher. To be accepted as teacher was the goal of my hopes. But I felt myself as much a learner as a teacher, I had come to India with everything to teach and nothing to learn. I stay to learn as well, and I believe I am a better man for having come into contact with the gentle heart of the East.

But is "teacher" the right word? I wonder if "introducer" isn't better? I spoke to a Hindu student one night in the after-meeting of a series and asked him if he didn't want to know Christ. "Yes," he said, eagerly, "but I do not know how to go to him. I need someone to introduce me to him." I suggested that I should love to introduce him to my Master. I saw quite vaguely then what is clear to me now: my chief business and chief joy is to introduce men and women to this Christ of the Indian Road.

If I do that, I must know him myself, and that means much. "Have you seen Jesus?" a Hindu lawyer asked me one day. I could not glibly reply, but slowly said, "Yes, I believe I have." "Then," said he, "you have found something that I have not yet found. I must get it."

To know him, to introduce him—this is my task.

There is a beautiful Indian marriage custom that dimly illustrates our task in India, and where it ends. At the wedding ceremony the women friends of the bride accompany her with music to the home of the bridegroom. They usher her into the presence of the bridegroom—that is as far as they can go, then they retire and leave her with her husband. That is our joyous task in India: to know Him, to introduce Him, to retire—not necessarily geographically, but to trust India with the Christ and trust Christ with India. We can only go so far—he and India must go the rest of the way.

India is beginning to walk with the Christ of the Indian Road. What a walk it will be!

www.ingramcontent.com/pod-product-compliance
Lightning Source LLC
Chambersburg PA
CBHW011916211224
19361CB00013B/44